Mike Erre

Why the Bible Matters

HARVEST HOUSE PUBLISHERS

EUGENE, OREGON

Cover photo © pixinstock / iStockphoto.com

Cover by Left Coast Design, Portland, Oregon

Mike Erre: Published in association with the literary agency of Mark Sweeney & Associates, Bonita Springs FL 34135.

Published in association with the Conversant Media Group, PO Box 3006, Redmond WA 98007.

WHY THE BIBLE MATTERS
Copyright © 2010 by Mike Erre
Published by Harvest House Publishers
Eugene, Oregon 97402
www.harvesthousepublishers.com

Library of Congress Cataloging-in-Publication Data

Erre, Mike
  Why the Bible matters / Mike Erre.
    p. cm.
  Includes bibliographical references (p.).
  ISBN 978-0-7369-2730-7 (pbk.)
  1. Bible—Introductions. I. Title.
  BS475.3.E84 2010
  220.6'1—dc22

                                                      2009046991

Download a Deeper Experience

Mike Erre is part of a faith-based online community called Conversant Life.com. At this website, people engage their faith in entertainment, creative arts, science and technology, global concerns, and other culturally relevant topics. While you're reading this book, or after you have finished reading, go to www.conversantlife.com/mikeerre and use these icons to read and download additional material from Mike that is related to the book.

 Resources: Download study guide materials for personal devotions or a small-group Bible study.

 Video: Click on this icon for interviews with Mike and video clips on various topics.

 Blogs: Read through Mike's blogs and articles and comment on them.

 Podcasts: Stream ConversantLife.com podcasts and audio clips from Mike.

conversant life .com

engage your faith

To Seth
May God give us a lifetime of surprises together.

Acknowledgments

Thanks to...

Justina	for putting up with the madness
Stan, Bruce, Mark, and Peter	for your vision
R.H.	for grace and encouragement
Gary, Todd, Stacy, and Chad	for being "in it" with me
Steve	for being a breath of fresh air
M.B.	for being such an example
J.P.	for help, advice, and perspective
Terry and Gene	for believing in me and this project
Anya	for laughing at bad jokes

Contents

PART I
The Story We Find Ourselves In

Introduction:
Why the Bible (Still) Matters

*Ivan Illich was once asked what is the most
revolutionary way to change society. Is it violent
revolution or is it gradual reform? He gave a
careful answer. Neither. If you want to change
society, then you must tell an alternative story.*

TIM COSTELLO

On September 18, 2008, my wife and I found out the child we were expecting (our third) had Down syndrome. At 22 weeks, we were given the option of terminating the pregnancy. We also discovered that roughly 92 percent of people receiving the same diagnosis at the same time choose that option.

How does a person make a decision like this? I have since reflected a lot on the journey Justina and I took as we went from hearing the news to seeing Seth born three months later. For us, abortion was never an option. We grieved and were frustrated, but ultimately we would receive Seth however God would give him to us. But I also can empathize with those for whom the thought of raising a Down syndrome child was too much. (Of course, this doesn't justify their decision to abort, but I can relate to the feelings of being overwhelmed.)

What guides us in moments like these, when reality comes crashing into our lives without any thought of our preferences or desires? Is it pure self-interest that guides us? What maximizes pleasure or minimizes pain? What will other people think of our decision? What does Oprah or Dr. Phil or Dr. Laura think we should do?

I am convinced that most of us live according to a narrative, a story that governs our lives and gives them structure, form, and shape (more about this later). These narratives answer the basic questions about us: Who are we? Where did we come from? Why are we here? Where are we going? What is right? What is wrong? Can we even know these things?

We carry these narratives unconsciously until we encounter situations that don't fit into the ways we normally make decisions and choices and deliberate about our lives. In those situations, we are exposed. We may normally give lip service to creeds, mutter token prayers, or quote pithy and inspiring slogans, but such things ring hollow in a crisis. The flannel-board Bible stories we heard in Sunday school aren't adequate for the demands of adult life.

Then we discover what kind of story we are actually living by. When we are sick of our spouses and want to divorce, when we can earn a ton of money by taking a few moral shortcuts, when a diagnosis puts life in perspective, or when every fiber in our being yearns to hurt those who hurt us—that's when we find out what the narrative of our lives really is.

One of the many reasons the Bible still matters is that it reveals the weaknesses of the stories of our world and tells an alternative story. And it is not just any story; it is the true story.

The scriptures paint a picture of an alternative reality, of life in another world. In this world, God raises the dead and breathes hope into every corner of the universe. In this world, all things are possible with God—virgin births, miraculous healings, cosmic warfare. Life is infused with holiness and worth, and people are valued far beyond their ability to produce or consume. In this reality, blessings can come disguised as the loss of the job, a health crisis, or the birth of a special-needs baby. Justina and I have come to believe that Jesus turns the world upside down, and as a result, we think and choose, live and spend, and act and relate differently than we would otherwise. Years of reading and studying the scriptures and listening to sermons about the Bible have formed us into people who (usually) believe that the world it describes is the real world. Without such a basis, I don't know how we would have made our decision about Seth.

So why does the Bible matter? Why should we wade through the *begats* (as my mom calls them) of this ancient book when we already have so little time to do so? My answer is simply this: The Bible reveals the world as it really is. It is not (primarily) a theological textbook, a body of laws and regulations, or a collection of nice moral stories. It is a story that presents a different way of seeing the world and our lives in it.

The biblical narrative is true, good, and right. It makes sense of our experience and the experiences of others. But the art and science of seeing the Bible in this way has been mostly lost in the Western world. Here, the Bible is been dissected, analyzed, cataloged, and categorized nearly into irrelevance. Even believers approach the Bible somewhat as if it were a museum artifact—pulling it off a shelf now and again, looking at and admiring it—rather than the dynamic and dangerous word of God it claims to be. Christians seem to spend a lot of time and energy defending the Bible when they could be engaging it in a consistently honest and meaningful way.

Ultimately the biblical narrative is subversive to all other narratives. In other words, it serves as the fundamental basis for everything else. We insist that the Bible gives a truer, more accurate account of what is going on in our seemingly unraveling world than do our advertisers, politicians, and journalists.

Looking at the scriptures this way helps us to be intellectually honest—grappling deeply with questions about the inspiration, transmission, and interpretation of the text—while at the same time holding a high view of the Bible. I believe we can hold the tremendous unity and clarity of the Bible—the story of God's quest to redeem what He has made—in tension with the utter mystery of many of its parts. But to do this we need to reframe our view of what the Bible is and what we expect it to do.

Writing a book about the Bible feels a bit like digging a hole in my backyard and calling it the Grand Canyon. Regardless of how well I dig or how deep I go, my hole will never compare to the real thing. So here's my first piece of advice for you: Buy yourself a Bible and begin to read it if you haven't already. When you read the Bible humbly and honestly, it speaks for itself. You don't need to go to seminary, learn Greek or Hebrew, or ask an expert in order to understand the basic message. Anyone anywhere can pick up the scriptures and benefit.

But at the same time, the Bible is clearly more than it first appears. Far beyond a list of do's and don'ts, rights and wrongs, laws and commandments, it combines poetry, narrative, parable, apocalypse, gospel, and more into a combustible mix that can be used for great good or great harm. Skinheads and cultists appeal to the Bible for authority, as do great social and moral reformers. The Bible is at the center of faith for billions of people, and it still stands as the most dramatic, controversial, and inspiring piece of literature ever put together.

And yet for all its acclaim, the Bible remains a mystery to most of us. Yes, all of us can pick it up and benefit, but we can also spend the rest of our lives plumbing its depths and never reach the bottom. From the prophets' cryptic mutterings to the bizarre images in Revelation, the Christian scriptures present us with a paradox: How do we reconcile the lofty view of the Bible espoused by millions—that it is the inerrant and inspired word of God—with the reality that most of us don't really understand what it is, let alone what it says. Many of us simply don't try to read, study, or apply the Bible much at all. For all of our defending of the Bible, few of us take it seriously.

How can you take the Bible seriously? That's the subject of this book.

The True Story of the World

*The Christian story claims to be the true
story about God and the world.*

N.T. WRIGHT

Reality can only be partially attacked by logic.

FRIEDRICH DURRENMATT

My kids love jigsaw puzzles. That means I have had to learn to love puzzles too. I have discovered what any puzzle lover already knows: The most important part of the puzzle is the box top, which shows the big picture. Of course, we still have to do the hard work of placing the individual pieces together, but the box top gives us a general sense of how best to proceed.

Many of us approach the Bible as a bunch of individual puzzle pieces without any real sense of how they all fit together. We lack a box top that gives us the big picture. And without it, many of us struggle to make sense of the individual pieces. How do Jesus' words to love our enemies fit with the psalmist's request for God to dash his enemies' children against the rocks? Or how do the obscure and esoteric words and pictures of the prophets fit into the straightforward history of Acts? We have a vague sense that it should all fit together, but we don't know how.

So for the most part, we approach the Bible individualistically and atomistically. We read the gospels as individual and independent stories about Jesus and rarely consider the way they are edited and arranged. We read about the people in the Old Testament—Moses or Joseph or Esther or David—without any sense of how these stories advance the grand narrative of God's mission to redeem what He has made.

We may approach the book of Proverbs for practical guidance and advice about living, parenting, running a business, or dating. Others of us may turn to 1 Corinthians 13, Psalm 23, the Beatitudes, or the Lord's Prayer for comfort and inspiration. In fact, if your Bible doesn't include a list of what passages to read when you are depressed or worried or sad, you can find one at the nearest Christian bookstore. Still others of us love the intellectual challenge of unraveling the paradoxes in the Bible. What's the deal with blood sacrifice or predestination or hell? How does Paul's emphasis on faith fit with James' emphasis on works? Was there one blind man or two, and did Jesus encounter him (or them) while entering Jericho or leaving it? Those who read the Bible this way often look for a verse or story that will support their position.

But all of these approaches ignore the fact that although the Bible was written by many authors over hundreds of years, it presents one unified story—the story of God's creative and redemptive work in the world.[1] And it is precisely in understanding the Bible as one overarching narrative that all the rest of it begins to make sense. The problem with approaching the Bible in one of these other ways—for guidance, challenge, or inspiration—is that we use the Bible for what *we* want and don't allow God to use it to form and shape us according to what He wants.

We must move beyond reading the Bible for our purposes and learn to receive it according to the authors' intentions. We must learn to read the Bible as it is presented to us and not always in the way we want, molding and shaping it to reinforce our own preferences, prejudices, or desires. And to do *that,* we must see the Bible as a unified whole.

Yes, this story does consist of many other stories, but each smaller story advances the narrative arc of the whole.

This story develops over a long time, so we must continually reconnect each individual part—a proverb, song, poem, prophecy, or parable—to the whole. Further, as the story advances, each scene sheds new light on the earlier parts of the story.

One Story or Many?

I grew up hearing that the Bible is composed of many kinds (or genres) of literature: poetry and history, parable and sermon, letter and genealogy, oracles and prophecies, songs and visions. And of course, there were stories. Loads of them. Stories about Jesus, about David and Goliath, Noah and the ark, Joseph and the famine in Egypt... But it never occurred to me to ask if the whole Bible fell into its own category. Now I believe it does. It is one unified story that is made up of a lot of individual pieces and parts, and the overriding narrative of the biblical story shapes these individual parts. The songs, letters, and genealogies make the most sense when we see them embedded in the larger plotline—the narrative thread that binds together the authors, books, and types of literature in the Bible.

That the Bible is one story should be apparent simply from the way it begins in Genesis with God creating the heavens and earth (Genesis 1:1) and ends in Revelation with the new heaven and new earth (Revelation 21:1). The biblical story works, of course, on many different levels and with many types of literature within it. Much of it doesn't read like a typical story, but such material makes full sense only within the broader story line.

Far from being a random mix of law, prophecy, poem, theology, and history, the Bible is a unified and progressively unfolding drama—the story of God's intention and work to redeem and restore what He has made—and each individual bit must be understood in the context of the whole. And God intends that whole story to be the framework that guides His people as they live, relate, and work in the world.

Every culture has an overriding narrative that shapes its collective consciousness. When we look at only the individual pieces of the Bible, we may misunderstand or distort them. Or we may remain myopic and individualistic, using the Bible for our purposes instead of submitting to God's purposes for us in it. But the greatest danger is that we will continue to live by other stories and interpret the Bible according to *them*. And that's a problem because most of the dominant values and narratives of the Western world are antithetical to the narrative of scripture. Make no mistake: We do live our lives according to a narrative (a framework, or a way of looking at the world) even if we cannot articulate what it is. So the question is not *whether* we live according to some overriding narrative but rather which one. Our stories shape us, and we shape our stories. The people of God have been called out of the patterns and narratives of this world and into something far truer, richer, and deeper—the story of God and His work in the world.

Our modern Western stories are so engrained in our minds that we naturally use them to interpret the biblical story. These other (misleading) stories are insidious because they are so foundational to the way we look at ourselves and the world. We rarely notice them, let alone call them into question. But that is precisely what we must do, for the Bible assumes (and the earliest Christians believed) that it alone tells the true story of our world.

Stories and Truth

Looking at the Bible this way may feel a bit odd to some of us because we grew up approaching the scriptures in search of timeless truth and doctrinal propositions. And certainly the Bible contains truth and doctrine and more besides. But those truths and propositions are housed in a narrative structure. They are not presented to us as abstract ideas disconnected from time, place, or culture. Just the opposite, in fact. A narrative arc (or structure) connects the many movements within the Bible. Our modern obsessions with doctrinal and theological fastidiousness have

blinded many of us to the rich images, allusions, symbols that permeate the Bible because of our search for the truth (or moral or point)
behind the story. In our never-ending quest for the bottom line, we
miss the significance of the journey along the way.

For instance, Jesus didn't describe God's love with three principles
in alliteration. He told a story about a man who had two sons. When
asked about loving one's neighbor, He told the story of the Good Samaritan. He used images (pearls, seeds, nets, soil) and symbols (temple,
wind, bread) that were embedded in everyday Jewish life to communicate the truth about the kingdom of God.

Similarly, when God gave the Ten Commandments to the nation
of Israel at Mt. Sinai, He began by saying, "I am the LORD your God,
who brought you out of Egypt, out of the land of slavery." The commandments that God gave Israel are not abstracted tidbits of morality.
Instead, they are connected to an event that was very fresh in their
minds—the powerful work of God to deliver them from Egypt. That
story connected the commandments to the nation and to God. The
God who spoke to the Israelites and commanded them to worship and
obey is the same God who led them out of Egypt and promised to
establish the nation in the Promised Land. Israel's God can be identi-
fied only by telling this story.

In the Old Testament, God's name and the story of His works go
together. The Bible does not allow for disembodied, theoretical truths
floating out there in creeds and doctrinal statements; it is rooted and
grounded in history through and through. It deals with particular
characters and events unfolding over real time and real places.

So when I say the Bible matters because it tells an alternative story,
I am not suggesting that the Bible is a fable, myth, or fairy tale. On the
contrary, I have become convinced that we are impoverished because we
have *reduced* the Bible down to propositions, steps, and principles. It is
so much bigger and deeper and truer than that. The Bible is presented
to us as a story for a reason, and I want to bring a needed correction
to our fascination with defending, defining, and "doctrinalizing" (I

needed another *d* word) at the expense of the rich and varied literary forms and structures that communicate at least as much truth as do propositions. New Testament scholar N.T. Wright highlights the nature and importance of stories:

> When we examine how stories work in relation to other stories, we find that human beings tell stories because this is how we perceive, and indeed relate to, the world... A story...is, if we may infer from the common practice of the world, universally perceived as the best way of talking about the way the world actually is... If Jesus or the evangelists tell stories, this does not mean that they are leaving history or theology out of the equation and doing something else instead.[2]

Why a Story?

Beyond a rule book, a systematic theology textbook, or a collection of inspiring sayings, the Bible presents itself to us as a story that describes the way the things really are. Stories, simply by virtue of their form, come to us less directly and immediately than propositional statements or doctrinal creeds. Stories, like those things, can either be true or false, but unlike them, stories leave room for our participation. God could have revealed Himself to us in any number of ways, but He chose to do it through narrative. We can reflect a bit on why He chose story as opposed to anything else.

Younger generations don't need to be convinced of the power of story. In their world, a cold, logical, abstract argument holds little value. They intuitively embrace imagination, mystery, ambiguity, and tension. Something is lost, of course, in the transition from more classically rational ways of understanding and discoursing, but much more is gained. When we read the Bible as a story, we allow it to speak for itself. On the other hand, when we argue about whether Adam and Eve had belly buttons, the message of the Bible can't get a word in edgewise. Stories are rational in their own way. They convey truth as do propositions, but they gain greater hearing these days.

How We Know Each Other

Stories are the most common way people relate to each other. When two people go on their first date and begin to get to know each other and share themselves with each other, they don't read each other's résumé. They tell stories about where they grew up and what they like to do. In cultures all over the world, stories are handed down from parents to children and repeated around the dinner table or campfire, reinforcing values, ideals, norms, and structures. They are the most accessible forms of speech: Young or old, educated or illiterate, anyone can savor a good story. In this digital age, where mountains of important or trivial information come to us in the form of raw data, stories help make sense of the overall scheme of things. For all our sophistication and expertise, we remain unsure of how best to run our lives. We need a narrative that speaks the truth about who we are, who God is, and why life is the way it is.

Stories reveal things to us in ways nothing else can. Propositions tell us things; stories show them to us. They draw us into relationship and open up new worlds to us in ways that textbooks or rule books never can. In the Bible, *knowing* is always relational. When the Bible says that Adam knew his wife, it doesn't mean that Adam could list Eve's interests, but rather that Adam and Eve knew each other sexually and thus intimately and personally. The scriptures always assume that to *know* something is to know it with both the head and the heart. The two are always inseparably connected.

The Bible is God revealing Himself—showing us what He is like—in ways that transcend merely telling us (in an informational way) about His nature. This is not like the way we engage a textbook on mathematics or a dusty tome about copyright law. No, this is encountering a person in the pages of a text. The Bible is revelatory, not just informational. Story is the only form that allows for such personal engagement. When Jesus taught about the kingdom, He never gave a textbook definition. Instead, He told stories and parables that illumined those who had ears to hear and hearts to receive the truth He revealed.

It's a Big World After All

Stories enlarge our world. Suppose you lived your whole life in a small village in the bottom of a valley that was surrounded by mountains. Suppose also that you were never allowed to climb the surrounding hillsides and had never heard anyone talk about life outside the village. Once you become an adult, however, you decide to see for yourself what lies beyond your small piece of the world. Imagine how you feel when you climb one of the peaks and discover that you live on a small island in the middle a vast ocean dotted by other islands. As your view stretches endlessly from horizon to horizon, you realize the world is much bigger than what you had previously known. Your village never looks the same after that. The limited perspective you once lived by is gone forever.

This is what stories do to us—they open up whole new worlds, provide us with unique and dissimilar perspectives, and cause us to look at our own lives a bit differently. They pull us out of ourselves and into a larger universe, stretching our imaginations and lives beyond their original shape. And this is also what the Bible does—it opens up a new and yet strangely familiar world of creation and conflict, angels and demons, sin and redemption. Beyond what we have learned (or figured out on our own), the scriptures open up a world with God, a world in which all things are possible.

The Bible is not one story among many stories; it is *the* story, of which all others are but faint echoes. Stories enlarge our world, and the biblical story most of all.

We are not accustomed to thinking about the Bible this way. We talk of "bringing the Bible to life" or "making the Bible relevant to our lives" as if our lives were large and the Bible should fit into them. But that is exactly the opposite of what is really the case. The Bible is the vast, true world, and our tiny, sin-constricted lives desperately need to fit into *that*. The scriptures crack open our narcissistic shells and expose us to a "God-bathed world," to use Dallas Willard's beautiful phrase. The world of the Bible is far larger than the world of television and the Internet. This is the fundamental change many of us must make: to quit trying to fit the Bible into our lives and begin seeing our lives in it.

You're Invited

Stories invite us to participate. The parable of the prodigal son (Luke 15) may be the most well-known story Jesus told. A father has two sons, the younger of which demands his inheritance in advance. Inexplicably, the father acquiesces to his son's wishes, and soon the son is off blowing his wealth on what the Bible politely calls "wild living." As we all know, the son eventually becomes destitute, returns to his senses, and makes the journey home. The father sees his son in the distance, runs to embrace him, and throws a party to celebrate his homecoming. We then meet an older son, who, resentful at the party thrown in honor of his irresponsible brother, refuses to join in the celebration. The story ends with the father pleading with the older son, and then...

That's it. No resolution, no happy ending. No sudden twist, no big surprise. Jesus simply ends the parable right there. Jesus told two other parables before this one, all to answer Pharisees who criticized Him for spending too much time with "sinners." I believe Jesus ends His story in this way precisely so the Pharisees might find themselves in it. The parable is actually about two lost sons, not just one. The younger son's rebellion is not the only issue or even the main issue; the pride, self-righteousness, and ingratitude of the older, law-keeping brother causes him to be lost as well. The story ends without resolution. The ending is up to each of us.

Good stories leave much to the imagination so we can find ourselves in them. They don't give us all the details or fill in all the blanks.

Stories allow us to continue the drama in our heads and hearts. They invite us to identify with their characters, feel the weight of their emotions, and imagine ourselves in their world.

What is true of the parable is true of the Bible as a whole. When we read it properly, the Bible pulls us out of ourselves and invites (sometimes demands) participation in the world it describes. Our attempts, then, on getting a bit of the Bible (or God, for that matter) into our lives is totally misguided. The scriptures draw us in to meet God on His terms, and its narrative form as well as its overall narrative arc (God working to redeem fallen humanity and restore creation) calls for our involvement in it.

How do we teach children the Bible? We tell them stories: Noah and his ark, David and the giant, Daniel and the lions, Jonah and the whale, Mary and her baby, Peter on the water, and Jesus. The Bible allows our kids to enter into its world through the stories it tells. Or to use another example, when we attend a funeral, how do we celebrate the life of someone we loved? We tell stories. We don't just talk in abstract terms about the person. We say, "Do you remember the time…?" In this way, we are drawn into the loved one's life again and again. Kenneth E. Bailey, an author who has spent decades in the Middle East studying the New Testament, explains the way Bible stories do their work:

> A biblical story is not simply a "delivery system" for an idea. Rather, the story first creates a world and then invites the listener to live in that world, to take it on as part of who he or she is… In reading and studying the Bible, ancient tales are not examined merely in order to extract a theological principle or ethical model.[3]

Going Deeper

Stories have layers of meaning. Stories are always embedded in a cultural context, yet they transcend context better than any other literary form. If we return to the parable of prodigal son, we can read it and grasp its main point without any knowledge whatsoever of first-century Jewish culture. Stories reach far beyond their cultural setting.

When we do study the cultural context, however, we notice detail and nuance in the parable that would otherwise escape us. For instance, in that day, the younger son's request was a clear statement that the money meant more to him than his father did. In effect, he was saying he wished his father were dead. And the father's acceptance of the arrangement was equally as scandalous. Finally, in Jewish culture, the head of a household would never *run,* so the father's dramatic and hurried response to his son's return is even more surprising. Like King David, who "defiled himself" centuries earlier by dancing before the Lord, this father was so filled with joy, he never noticed (or didn't care) that he humiliated himself.

You get the picture. Stories can translate between cultures effectively, and yet knowledge of those cultures allows us to find new shades of meaning and significance that deepen our understanding of the stories and their impact on our lives.

We may read about the plagues God sent against Pharaoh and Egypt and understand that God was releasing Israel from bondage. Yet when we learn a bit about ancient Egyptian religion, we discover that God targeted each plague at a particular Egyptian deity. (That's why God says, "I will bring judgment on all the gods of Egypt" in Exodus 12:12.) Far from being natural occurrences or random series of judgments, the plagues display God's greatness and power over the false gods of Egypt. The main point of the Exodus narrative stays the same, but the cultural details add depth and richness to the story and deepen our appreciation of God.

The Subversive Nature of Storytelling

Stories can be incredibly subversive. The most powerful journalism is storytelling. I can read statistics about the rise in autism, or I can meet Brian, a sweet five-year-old who lives in our area who struggles to interact socially with his peers and is still learning how to talk.

Which is more moving, the statistics or the story? The story, of course. As Ivan Illich so powerfully states, telling an alternative story is the surest way to revolution. N.T. Wright agrees:

> Human life, then, can be seen as grounded in and consti-tuted by the implicit or explicit stories which humans tell themselves and one another... Stories thus provide a vital framework for experiencing the world. They also provide a means by which views of the world may be challenged... Stories are, actually, particularly good at modifying or sub-verting other stories and their worldviews. Where head-on attack would certainly fail, the parable hides the wisdom of the serpent behind the innocence of the dove, gaining entrance and favour which can then be used to change assumptions which the hearer would otherwise keep hidden away for safety.[4]

Isn't that what we read in the book of Acts as the disciples begin to announce the resurrection of Jesus of Nazareth? As they testify to the reality of Jesus as the fulfillment of Israel's hopes, they (consciously or not) begin to subvert Jewish narratives of the day, such as these: There is no Messiah to be expecting, there is no resurrection of the dead, and Rome must be defeated by strength of arms. When Paul began his missionary efforts in Roman Asia Minor and insisted that Jesus is *Lord,* he boldly co-opted a title that the Caesars had reserved for themselves. The imagery of the book of Revelation was also sedi-tious. It suggested that much of the propaganda of Roman emperor worship was misplaced and even demonic, that Jesus is greater than earthly rulers, and that He alone is Lord.

The Bible is the most subversive story ever written. As we look at each stop along the narrative arc of the scriptures, we'll see how the biblical story indicts the major narratives that govern our lives as West-erners in the twenty-first century and offers something much better, truer, and larger.

The Story God Tells

Of course, some stories are good and true, and others are bad and false. Stories also differ in their purposes. Some entertain, some teach, some remind, some provide warnings. And some stories reveal the foundation and base of our worldview. They attempt to answer the big questions of life. These stories are the most important ones even though we don't often think about them.

The Bible offers the truest story of the whole world—all of life, history, experience, culture, and civilization are encompassed in its pages. To see the Bible as the truest story is not to say that the story helps us function well or that it was passed down to us merely as a cultural inheritance. The scriptures must be taken seriously because they claim to tell us the true story from the creation of the universe all the way to its re-creation. Not one moment is left out of its pages. The content of the Bible lies at the very core of reality. This is the way the world really is.

If we don't read the scriptures this way, if we try to fit them into our individual or collective modern stories, we lose the full reality of God and His work in our world. Our world shrinks as well. The story of the Bible is the story of enlargement, not reduction. In God's world, a teenage virgin wakes up one day to discover she will give birth to the promised Messiah, a lowly fisherman becomes a cornerstone of the church, murderers and prostitutes turn into saints, and our ordinary world becomes a vessel for the holy. Modern narratives seek to reduce us, making us out to be nothing more than our synapses, impulses, or environmental conditioning. The scriptures call us into a much larger world, and in so doing, they beckon us beyond the reach of our wills and experiences.

Parts of this story are repeated in worship and liturgy, recited in creeds, and reenacted in baptism and communion. But to get the full measure, we need the whole of the Bible from beginning to end. The scriptures narrate the essential story we live in as God's people in the world. We can proclaim our belief that the Bible is God's word, but until we allow it to define us to this degree, our hollow words are nothing more than lip service.

The Bible was written by many different authors across hundreds of generations and is now organized into 66 different books. To get a handle on its great and grand story and trace its narrative arc, we must utilize the largest biblical categories we can find. We can delineate these categories in different ways, but some consistency in the overall picture remains. The scriptures present a multiact drama of salvation that unifies the Bible as a whole story. The stories about Jesus, for instance, are presented in continuity with the stories about Israel and make sense only in that narrative framework. Jesus cannot be abstracted from the rest of the biblical story. "As the fulfillment of creation and the story of Israel, Jesus initiates the life of the church that witnesses to the coming new creation."[5]

Very simply, the overall story line goes something like this: God creates the world and everything in it. His creatures rebel, allowing sin and death to mar all that God made. God is rescuing and restoring creation and will renew it completely sometime in the future.

At the beginning, the triune God created everything in the universe and declared it all to be good. Human beings, bearing the imprint of their Creator's image, were made for relationship (with God and each other) and dominion (caring for God's world). They originally existed in perfect harmony (right relationship) with God, creation, and each other (Genesis 1–2).

Sin entered the world when God's creatures rebelled against His good and gracious rule, subjecting all aspects of God's good creation (including people) to corruption and decay (Genesis 3–11).

God immediately began to redeem what sin had corrupted. He invited one man, Abram, to live again under His reign. From Abraham (as we know him now) came the nation of Israel, which foreshadows and leads up to God's saving work in Christ.

Jesus came to earth to inaugurate God's reinstituted kingdom, through which God will rescue the world and reinstitute His original intentions for it. The Creator of all things has now become the Redeemer, and through His life, death, and resurrection, Jesus of Nazareth accomplished for us what we could not do for ourselves. He announced that the redemptive work of God is present in the kingdom of God and is available to anyone who calls on Him. He reversed what resulted through our rebellion and frees us from the power and consequences of sin and death.

The Bible teaches that God's work in the world is comprehensive. He is seeking to restore all of creation to its original design and goodness. The salvation of individuals is the most important part, but it is not the whole of God's work. This teaching makes some people nervous, so let me clarify.

The biblical picture of restoration and renewal extends to all of creation. But that does not suggest that somehow the earth itself is divine (pantheism) or that all people everywhere will live with God in His new world (universalism). Rather, the scriptures reveal that human beings and the created world around them are tied together in sin and fallenness, in redemtion and restoration (Romans 8).

The through-line in each of these sections is the kingdom of God. I have suggested elsewhere that the kingdom is the major (but not only) way of framing God's work of redemption.[6] *The kingdom God* is a descriptive name for His reign and rule over His people and eventually over all creation. Many of the covenants of the Bible are (or will be) fulfilled by the King in His kingdom. They define the relationship between the King and His subjects. As we enter into a relationship with God, we come under His governance, and His will is done. This rule and reign eventually will make its way through all of creation (more about that later).

N.T. Wright has offered his own overview of the central story of the Bible in the form of a five-act play, with most of the fifth act missing.[7] Bartholomew and Goheen suggest that Wright follows the structure of dramatic storytelling in the Western tradition:

> The five acts [of traditional Western dramatic storytelling] are generally organized this way: (1) The first act gives us essential background information, introduces the important characters, and establishes the stable situation that will be disrupted by the events about to unfold. (2) The first action begins usually with the introduction of a significant conflict. The middle of the play (3) is where the main action of the drama takes place. Here the initial conflict intensifies and grows ever more complicated until (4) the climax, or point of highest tension, after which that conflict must be resolved, one way or the other. After climax comes (5) the resolution, in which the implications of the climactic act are worked out for all the characters of the drama, and stability is restored.[8]

Wright uses this structure in his presentation of the overarching narrative of the Bible:

> Act 1: Creation
> Act 2: The Fall
> Act 3: Israel
> Act 4: Jesus
> Act 5: The Church

We live in the time of act 5, in which we improvise a suitable second scene, moving toward the conclusion God has revealed.[9]

Bartholomew and Goheen show that there is another act yet to come, in which Jesus returns and all things are made new.[10] Wright's analysis has been very helpful, but we will adopt a slightly different structure here. I see these acts in the narrative arc of the scriptures:

> Act 1: Creation
> Act 2: The Fall

Act 3: Redemption (of which Israel, Jesus, and the church are all parts)

Act 4: Restoration (the renewal of all creation)

The creation account tells us what is right and good about people and the created order. The record of the fall tells us what went wrong in us and in creation. Redemption is the process of reversing the effects of the fall and is the foundation of the Creator's plan to restore everything to its original goodness and rightness. Restoration (or renewal or new creation) is the perfect completion of God's work of redemption, in which all things are made new.

PART 2

The Story of God

The Beginning and the Time Before That

In the beginning God...

The majority of the Bible's story line describes God's work of redemption and restoration (Genesis 12–Revelation 22), but that doesn't mean that what happens prior to that is unimportant. In fact, people are often confused about our world and God's work in it because they neglect the first two parts of the biblical narrative: creation (Genesis 1–2) and the fall (Genesis 3–11). We cannot understand the full scope and beauty of God's salvation until we first understand God's original intent and the damage to God's good creation that resulted from the fall.

Surely the most important words in the history of human civilization are these: "In the beginning God..." This declaration—with no introduction, no argument for God's existence—sets the stage for all that follows. These four words open up limitless possibilities about the nature and reality of the universe. God's existence prior to the creation defines and shapes human culture.

We think of the Bible as a record of humanity's search for God, but the truth is precisely the opposite—it is a record of His pursuit of us. The Bible begins and ends with God. He is at the center of the universe; we are not. This is His story, and our stories find their proper place in His.

God did not need to create (as if He were lonely), nor did He create on a whim or by accident. Nothing compelled God to create. The rest of the Bible reveals that the one God (who is one being and also a relationship of Father, Son, and Spirit) creates as an overflow of the love and joy that characterize His internal, relational life (see John 17).

This is the God who "created the heavens and the earth." The kingdom of God is the domain over which God rules. In Genesis 1–2, we see God ruling over all and simply speaking the universe into existence. The power of His word is the power of creation. God creates all things ("the heavens and the earth") as an expression of His will.

God exists before (or outside of) His creation and brings all things into existence *ex nihilo*. He is the Creator-King who speaks His creation into existence from His throne and by His word. "In the beginning God created the heavens and the earth...And God said, 'Let there be light, and there was light.'"

Creator and creation are thus distinct from the outset. God is not in creation, nor is the universe simply part of His nature. The scriptures begin with the self-sufficient God commanding matter and energy however He wants to and with an end in mind. In Genesis 1–2, God's kingdom is established over and through creation—things are the way He wants them to be. Night and day, sea and land, sun and moon all obey His decrees. He sits over creation as King, not needing to create (as if He were deficient in some way until He did) but rather worthy of praise as Creator (see, for example, Revelation 4:11) because the universe stands as a testimony to His goodness and power (see Romans 1:20). As God creates, He names the parts of creation (such as land and sea) as an expression of His sovereignty over them.

Genesis 1

God fills and separates and in so doing creates order (seasons and days and years) and purpose. God's creation isn't static but instead includes possibilities—plants and seeds, trees and fruit, and animals that fly or swim or crawl on the ground, all able to reproduce "according to their kind."

The theme of separation runs through Genesis 1. God orders and delineates and defines. He creates limits and boundaries. Out of the chaos of verse 2, the dark and formless void, God brings order and purpose. Each day builds upon the next (probably in parallel). Living things are created according to their kind. This is another theme that runs throughout the creation account.

All of this is well-known to those of us familiar with the Bible. But unfortunately, most of our Christian stories do not start here. They usually start in Genesis 3 with the fall of humanity into sin, and they focus on God's redemption of what He has made. But the central features of the creation narratives are crucial, for they reveal God's original intent for His creation. They help us to see that people and the world they inhabit were specially designed to fulfill God's purposes. And this, as we'll see in the next chapter, has powerful ramifications for how we live today.

It Was Good

The creation story repeatedly declares that God was pleased with what He had made. Being created, then, is a good thing. This sounds pretty obvious, I know, but over the course of history, many of God's children have lost sight of this fundamental part of the story and decided that being physical was bad or unspiritual. Genesis begins with God delighting in what He has made, affirming its goodness for His purposes and according it worth because of His pleasure in it. When we read the Bible, we must keep this in mind: Creation is a reflection of God's goodness, order, and intelligence, so it is essentially good. Having a body is a good thing. Needing food, drink, air, love...all of this is good. Our material existence is and always has been good. The material world is not inferior to or somehow less spiritual than the rest of our existence.

All of God's world contained the rightness He intended for it. He embedded everything with integrity and an inclination toward His purposes. As a result, He receives honor in and through the entire created order and especially through humans' responsible and caring stewardship of the world.

Made in the Image

Genesis 1:26 records God speaking from His throne in the plural. Perhaps God is speaking to His heavenly court, the sea of angels gathered before Him. Or God could be using the *royal plural* or *plural of majesty,* as when the queen of England might say, "We are not amused." Or this could be a tantalizing hint of the plurality within God's one nature. That He is speaking to His court seems to me to be the more probable.

God made human beings in His own image. The poetic refrain of the first part of Genesis 1 ceases when God creates human beings. He made plants and animals "according to their kinds," but He made humans according to His own kind (that is, in His image and likeness). *Image* and *likeness* are two ways of saying the same thing. Though we are not divine ourselves, our nature is somehow like God's. And the immediate connection between our image and God's image is rulership: "Let them rule over the fish of the sea and the birds of the air, over the livestock, over all the earth." This mandate is repeated in verse 28: "God blessed them and said to them, 'Be fruitful and increase in number; fill the earth and subdue it. Rule over the fish of the sea and the birds of the air and over every living creature that moves on the ground.'"

Humanity alone shares God's image, especially in one important way. Kings and rulers in the ancient Near East placed sculptures and engravings of themselves in distant territories of their kingdoms to signify their dominion over those lands. Human beings bear God's image and likeness as representatives of His rule over the earth. We live under God's rule and extend it throughout creation as vice-regents or co-governors. He invites us to develop the possibilities latent within creation in ways that bring honor and glory to Him.

Our rule over the earth should parallel God's rule over us. We are responsible for the land, water, air, plants, animals, and other natural resources. Our part in the creation story is to care for the earth because in so doing we bring glory to the Creator and fulfill an essential part of our humanity. As God works for the good of humanity, so too humanity must work for the good of the created order. We steward or manage creation in ways that embody God's own care for and delight in the created order. Under His overarching dominion, we are given a small piece of dominion for our own. Bartholomew and Goheen put it this way:

> To be human means to have huge freedom and responsibility, to respond to God and to be held accountable for that response. Thus, a better way of expressing the concept of humankind's "dominion" over creation may be to say that we are God's royal stewards, put here to develop the hidden potentials in God's creation so that the whole of it may celebrate his glory.[1]

In other words, humans are called to steward creation in a way that advances God's reputation. We were given this work before the fall, so it is part of our original design. Our stewardship role reminds us that the world is not static; it is going somewhere, and the image of God in us includes the assignment to direct it toward God-honoring and beneficial ends. It also gives us a great range of volition and freedom as we fulfill this responsibility. God gave us moral, intellectual, emotional, and relational capacities so we could fulfill this calling.

The command has two parts. We fulfill the first part, "be fruitful and multiply," by building families, cities, governments, and businesses. The second part, "subdue the earth," doesn't mean that we should pillage, pollute, or strip-mine the world. Instead, we are to harness the natural world and steer it toward God-honoring, human-benefitting ends. We do this in many ways: We plant and cultivate, build and design, compose and paint.

This first command given to humanity is often called the *creation* or *cultural* mandate. God asks us to bring every single human cultural activity into His realm and rule. Art, politics, law, business... every aspect of human cultural existence provides an opportunity to honor God. As corulers with God and under God, we create just as He has created. In this way, we extend the blessedness of living under God's good dominion to every part of the world.[2]

Only human beings are made for this kind of relationship with God. We are also made to reflect God's character in this world. When God created us in His image, He placed us on this planet as a sign that it belongs to Him. It is His creation. We are created not only to relate to Him but also to rule the planet with the authority He has delegated to us. We are the signs that this is God's earth.

Male and Female He Created Them

Gender distinctions are essential parts of humanity. Image bearers are either male or female, but they express God's image most fully when they are in relationship. This leaves room for no subordination or inferiority between the sexes whatsoever. In fact, it demonstrates their complete equality before God.

Genesis 2

The first two chapters of Genesis complement each other. In Genesis 1, God is the *transcendent* Creator who speaks, and it is so. In Genesis 2, God is the *immanent* Creator who forms Adam from dust and breathes the breath of life into Him. When we compare these two accounts, we have an example of Hebrew parallelism. This is how the Hebrew mind works, so it is no surprise that the seven days of creation in Genesis 1 are followed by an extended narrative of the sixth day of creation in Genesis 2. This is an example of synthetic parallelism—the second account fleshes out the first account. Both climax or center in the creation of humankind.

Genesis 2:4 begins human history. The generations in Genesis 2:4

begin to live out the commands in Genesis 1: "This is the account [generations, history] of the heavens and the earth when they were created."

The Seventh Day

Creation doesn't end with the command to cultivate and care for the earth (the cultural mandate). God speaks six times on six days and then stops. He rests (ceases His work) not because He was tired, but because creation was complete. There is a time to work and a time when work is finished. God commands human beings to create just as He creates, and He commands us to rest as He rested (Exodus 31:16-17). Our work matters, but so does our resting from work. The Sabbath command reminds us that we are not indispensible to God and that we are to imitate the pattern of the Creator.

God rested on the seventh day. Creation is complete. Seven is the number of perfection. By resting on the seventh day, God blessed and sanctified it. This is foundational for the rhythm of human life and for Israel's imitation of God. He rests, and His people rest. By keeping the Sabbath, Israel expressed her unique destiny to live in harmony with the divine purpose and to witness this to the nations.

From the Dust

As we have seen, humans reflect God in a unique way. We are the only true union of the physical and the spiritual. God intended us to always be physical-spiritual hybrids and not primarily one or the other. Satan and demons and angels and God Himself are spiritual beings who can manifest themselves in the physical world (though their physicality is not essential to their nature like ours is). Animals and plants, on the other hand are physical; they don't share our soulish qualities. Only in humanity do the spiritual and material realms go together. We are made from dust, yet we have God's breath (or Spirit) in us, giving us life.

According to some other translations, God "breathed His spirit" into Adam. In Hebrew, this is fascinating wordplay. *Breath* and *spirit* share a common root, showing that the Hebrews understood that we are spiritual as well as physical. This spiritual part of us is one of the ways we reflect God's image. We are not merely collections of atoms or purely material brains. Something irreducibly immaterial is fundamental to who we are. David put it this way in Psalm 8:3-8:

> When I consider your heavens,
>   the work of your fingers,
> the moon and the stars,
>   which you have set in place,
> what is man that you are mindful of him,
>   the son of man that you care for him?
> You made him a little lower than the heavenly beings
>   and crowned him with glory and honor.
> You made him rule over the works of your hands;
>   you put everything under his feet:
> all flocks and herds,
>   and the beasts of the field,
> the birds of the air,
>   and the fish of the sea,
> all that swim the paths of the seas.

It Is Not Good for the Man to Be Alone

Genesis 1 tells the story of the creation of all things and the relationship between human beings and the world around them. Genesis 2, on the other hand, focuses on the relationship between the man and the woman and includes different but complementary details.

The man is made first. God forms him out of earth and breathes His life into him. He commands the man to work the garden and warns him not to eat the fruit from the mysterious tree of the knowledge of good and evil. Just as God had previously named the parts of creation, showing His sovereignty over it all, the man now names the animals, showing his delegated authority over the animal kingdom. God put him to sleep and creates woman because "it is not good for the man to be alone." This is the only thing that was not good before the fall (so far, everything has been "good" or "very good"). The woman is a suitable helper for the man and his work in the world.[3]

Woman is God's special creation. Man has a created loneliness; he is made for relationship, human as well as divine. This is the first negative thing in creation before the fall: "Then the LORD God said, 'It is not good for the man to be alone. I will make a helper suitable [or fit] for him'"(Genesis 2:18). Created loneliness is not a sign of sin. It is a divinely ordained need for companionship. This helper, who will be "fit for him," will be a companion, a friend, one who will be equal to him and with him.

The first scientific activity occurs when Adam classifies the animals by naming them (Genesis 2:20). He has authority over them, but none of them is a helper "fit for him." Our created loneliness is not solved in the animal kingdom. God then anaesthetizes Adam in verse 21. In a deep sleep, God takes one of his ribs, fashions a woman, and brings her to him. Notice the Hebrew parallelism in verse 23: "Bone of my bones, and flesh of my flesh; she will be called 'woman,' for she was taken out of man." God gives Adam a companion who is "fit for him." This is foundational for verses 24-25. We see the relationship that God designed for us and calls us to.

This passage highlights the relational aspects of the image of God in humanity. The man and woman enjoy close and intimate relationship with each other and with God. Our capacities for relationship are central to our humanity. Being alone is still not good. We were made to need each other and to live in peace with our Creator as personal beings.

Genesis 1–2 presents God as the eternal, self-sufficient Creator of all things, but He is not distant from what He has made. We see hints of His relational nature…

> when He decides to create humankind: "Let *us* make…"
> (Genesis 1:26)

when He speaks directly to the man and woman (Genesis 1:28)

when He walks among the garden in search of Adam and Eve (Genesis 3:8)

These glimpses show us God's intention not only to create but also to relationally interact with His creatures. God gives the first humans the privilege and responsibility of working the earth and caring for it, and He invites them into relationship with Him, their Creator and King. He created a garden for their pleasure (the Hebrew word *Eden* means "delight") and carefully structured the rest of creation for human life. In the opening creation account we see God's intent, design, and care for all that He has made.

At the essence of God's creative intent for the world is the Hebrew concept of *shalom*. In the Bible, that word is usually translated "peace," but it means much more than simply the absence of conflict. *Shalom* denotes a rich, integrated relational wholeness and unity. Cornelius Plantinga defines *shalom* this way:

> The webbing together of God, humans, and all creation in justice, fulfillment, and delight is what the Hebrew prophets call *shalom*. We call it peace, but it means far more than mere peace of mind or cease-fire between enemies. In the Bible, shalom means *universal flourishing, wholeness and delight...* Shalom, in other words, is the way things ought to be.[4]

The dimensions of *shalom* (the wholeness, peace, and harmony built into God's creation before the fall) in human beings were focused in four directions:

Inward: They had no sin, shame, or guilt.

Outward: They were naked and unashamed.

Upward: They had intimacy with God.

Downward: They directed creation toward God-honoring ends.

One Flesh and Not Ashamed

Wholeness and unity extend not only to relationship with God but also to human relationships. Marriage language is introduced and includes sexuality ("united to his wife") as an expression of joining the two into one. In fact, the Hebrew word translated *one* is the same word used to describe God's oneness in Deuteronomy 6:4: "Hear, O Israel: The LORD our God, the LORD is one." In some mysterious way, the joining of the man and woman imitates or even reflects the unity of God.

The narrative then moves on to report the intimacy and connection that Adam and Eve share. Their closeness is pictured in their nakedness and innocence.

Genesis 1–2 presents a vision of the original goodness of God's world. Untainted by sin, human beings live in personal relationships with God and each other. They are to cultivate the earth in a way that glorifies God and benefits them. Everything reflects His goodness and intention for it. The creation account is profound by itself, and its ramifications significantly contradict many of our modern stories, as we'll see in the next chapter.

The God-Absented World

*It is not so much what we don't know, but what
we think we know that obstructs our vision.*

Krister Stendahl

We live in a God-absented culture. In the big story of the last two centuries of Western culture, humankind has seemed to be able to make coherent sense out of human life on earth without reference to God. Our origin, purpose, nature, and experience can now be thought of in almost exclusively materialistic and mechanistic terms. Belief in the existence of an all-powerful, all-loving Creator, though still popular, is widely considered a cultural hangover, a purely sociological phenomenon of the masses that has little basis in reality. In fact, discussions of religion, morality, and ethics are now relegated to the area of personal belief, opinion, value, or preference. Religious knowledge is generally considered an oxymoron. Whole segments of society now function without reference to God. Entertainment, education, medicine, the sciences, technology, commerce, media…all of these often function with an entirely secular backdrop.

The World with God

Into this milieu, the creation narratives of Genesis speak an incredibly subversive word. In fact, Genesis 1–2 has always been subversive of other accounts of the world's origins. Many commentators hold that these poetic chapters (especially chapter 1) form a countercultural narrative that subverts other ancient Near East creation accounts.

The ancient Near Eastern world had many competing creation myths. The Jews were not the only people to adopt a story of the origins of the world and its people. Though Genesis 1–2 seems a bit strange to us, it was written in a cultural context significantly different from ours and served a polemical purpose: It directly contradicted the other origin stories circulating in the world.

For instance, Genesis 1 refers to the sun and moon not by their proper Hebrew names, but instead calls them "the greater light" and "the lesser light." Bartholomew and Goheen suggest this is because many ancient Near Eastern cultures considered the sun and moon to be objects of worship. The creation story deliberately assigns them a place among the created order. God alone is to be worshipped, and the sun and moon are merely instruments He created for His purposes.[1]

Similarly, the Creator God of Genesis 1–2 is nothing like the gods of the Babylonian creation story, the *Enuma Elish,* who create humanity to serve them and fulfill their desires. Instead, God creates humans in His image, gives them work to do (modeled after His own work), and invites them into relationship with Him.[2]

The Genesis creation account reminded the Israelites, who always lived among pagan peoples, that the God who delivered them from Egypt was the same God who created the heavens and the earth. Genesis, then, presented a reality that stood in stark contrast and opposition to the other origin stories at the time.

Genesis 1–2 goes beyond this polemical function, however, to present a vision of God's grand intention and design for the world. Regardless of one's view on the relationship between the Bible and current scientific teaching, it is abundantly apparent that there is a *design* to what God has made. There is order, purpose, and intention. God's creation has an ultimate end or goal (the Greek word *telos,* which philosophers have brought into the English language, describes this). We must understand this part of the narrative in order to appreciate the way it subverts the stories that govern twenty-first-century life.

The World Without God

As a result of the God-absented story that now dominates the Western world, many people live without any sense of telos (purpose or design). Evolutionary theory holds that the purpose for evolution is simply the survival and propagation of the species. Entertainment and media present us with a picture of life at its self-indulgent worst. If we buy into the story the news is telling, the greatest human goods are sex appeal, wealth, status, and fame. Education, once a stable purveyor of telos, has abandoned such notions and now promotes learning simply for the sake of learning. Materialism tells us that the only things that are real are the things we can see, hear, touch, taste, smell, or scientifically discover in the material world. Naturalism defines human beings as nothing more than particles and body parts—no immortal soul, no immaterial spirit, no mind beyond the neurotransmissions in our brains. We are simply the sum total of our pieces. Consumerism markets a happiness (leading to fulfillment and pleasure) based on the satisfaction of our desires. Humans were not designed with a telos in mind.

These three isms—materialism, naturalism, and consumerism—are the stories that govern Western life. They tell us who we are, where we have come from, where we are going, and what counts as a life well lived. While not officially housed under the category of religion, this all-encompassing story answers all of life's great religious questions for us. Who am I? I am an advanced mammal who will exist for a few years on this planet. Why am I here? I exist because human life evolved from simple cellular forms of life into increasingly complex arrays of particles and structures. In the absence of telos, everything goes. Nothing can be inherently better or worse than anything else. Where am I going? Wherever I want to. The future is open because medicine and technology, fueled by science, will eventually overcome every obstacle.

Atheist Bertrand Russell (1872–1970) gives an apt description of the implications of scientific naturalism:

> That man is the product of causes which had no prevision of the end they were achieving; that his origin, his growth, his hopes and fears, his loves and his beliefs are but the outcome of accidental collections of atoms; that no fire, no heroism, no intensity of thought and feeling, can preserve an individual life beyond the grave; that all the labors of the ages, all the devotion, all the inspiration, all the noonday brightness of human genius, are destined to extinction in the vast death of the solar system, and that the whole temple of man's achievement must inevitably be buried beneath the debris of a universe in ruins—all these things, if not quite beyond dispute, are yet so nearly certain that no philosophy which rejects them can hope to stand. Only within the scaffolding of these truths, only on the firm foundation of unyielding despair, can the soul's habitation henceforth be safely built.[3]

Though trumpeted as long-standing fact, these stories actually appeared on the human landscape relatively recently. Our contemporary worldview narratives are not the only way to see the world. They emerged in the Enlightenment of the seventeenth and eighteenth centuries and are fundamentally humanistic. People came to believe that through human reason, science, and technology alone, utterly apart from God, humanity could build a perfect world.

These stories gradually led to the secularization of Western culture. Craig Gay comments on the nature of secularization:

> [Secularization] is a subtle and largely inadvertent process in which religion—at least as it has traditionally been understood—forfeits its place in society. Secularization describes a process in which religious ideas, values, and institutions lose their public status and influence and eventually even their plausibility in modern societies.[4]

The cost of the gradual secularization of our dominant narratives has been high. Though in twenty-first-century America we are far better off than our parents and grandparents according to any measure, including life expectancy, quality of life, availability of heath care, wealth, and leisure time, we are far less happy than they. Fewer and fewer of us experience a deep sense of well-being on a day-to-day basis.[5] Without telos to human life, we have ceased living from and for something bigger than ourselves and instead live simply to fulfill our desire. The consequence of this vapid pursuit, according to Philip Cushman, is an "empty self."

> The empty self is filled up with consumer goods, calories, experiences, politicians, romantic partners, and empathetic therapists... [The empty self] experiences a significant absence of community, tradition, and shared meaning...a lack of personal conviction and worth, and it embodies the absences as a chronic, undifferentiated emotional hunger.[6]

The Possibility of Something Else

Genesis 1–2 opens up the possibility of revelation from something outside the physical universe. These chapters suggest that our world must find an explanation for its existence and nature outside of its own matter, forms, and processes. If God exists and did create, our view of the world must become much bigger to accommodate the possibility of His work in the world.

If we are to believe the underlying truths of the Genesis narrative, we must admit the reality of telos in the universe. Whether we believe God used evolutionary processes or created in an instant, we can be confident that purpose, order, design, and intelligence stand behind the created world. And this telos is grounded in the creative purposes of the God we encounter in the opening pages of the Bible.

The biblical account of creation contradicts our modern myths at every point. Against materialism, Genesis 1–2 holds that the world of particles, elements, and energy is not the only stuff of the universe. The spiritual world is also a real part of the universe even though our physical senses can only give us hints of it.

Against materialism, the creation story portrays humanity as a physical-spiritual hybrid. Created from dust, yet imbued with the very breath (or Spirit) of the living God, human beings are neither fully physical (like animals, without souls) nor fully spiritual (like angels, who lack physical bodes as an essential part of their nature). Rather, we are both physical and spiritual. We cannot be reduced to simply the physical processes in our bodies, nor are we spirits trapped in physical shells. According to the scriptures, we stand at the pinnacle of God's good creation. This is not cause for boasting, but for thanksgiving, stewardship, and responsibility.

Against consumerism, the Genesis account declares that humanity was created *for* something. We are not accidents or products of time plus blind mutation and chance. Because we are the creation of intelligence and design, we are also the creation of purpose, or telos, as we have been describing. We are meant to function in certain ways, and these ways are central to human flourishing. The opening chapters of Genesis describe not only our creation but also our telos—God's intention for us. We find our telos not in our self-governance or pleasure but in the reality of God's intentions for us.

Created for What?

The modern world frowns on the idea of telos (purpose, function, and intention). Telos implies a norm or standard against which human nature and life can be measured. And the very act of measuring (against whatever standard) is offensive to contemporary culture.

But if the creation narrative is the true story of the origins of the world, then it reveals God's intentions for human beings, offensive or not. His intentions in designing and creating us should govern our self-understandings. But so much of the creation story inescapably conflicts with the stories that govern most of twenty-first-century life.

Because God created the world, telos exists, and the life lived under God's good rule will be the life of true human flourishing. The good life is the life lived according to God's purposes and order. Morality is likewise only properly situated within the creation story. Right and wrong, evil and goodness make no sense according to the three isms underlying the narrative our world currently accepts. What is good turns out to be identical to whatever works toward God's purposes in creation. What is evil is whatever works against them.

Community

Human beings are impossibly relational creatures, designed to need each other. We were made in the image of a relational God, so our need for community reflects that aspect of His nature. We should not miss the significance of the statement God makes about Adam in Genesis 2:18: "It is not good for the man to be alone. I will make a helper suitable for him." Imagine that! Adam had an absolutely unblemished relationship with God. He enjoyed a free-flowing exchange with his Creator that we can hardly image. And yet, even though nothing hindered his relationship with God—no sin, shame, guilt, fear, or hiding—he still was not complete. He lacked another of his own kind, so God created woman and brought her to Adam.

This highlights the pervasive human need to connect. People will use any invention—an Xbox 360 console, a personal computer, or bits and bytes of Internet data—to relate to each other. We can't help ourselves. Nor should we. But much of modern life stresses individualism (which is different from individuality)—individual rights, preferences, and obligations at the expense of more communal ways of living and seeing the world. The church is not immune. We often value a personal relationship with Jesus much more than the Bible does. Those who suggest that all we need is God are well-intentioned but incorrect. Adam had as much of God as anyone could have, yet God declared that it was not good that he was alone. We were made to need each other. Very few things can carry us joyfully through the ups and downs of life in our fallen world, but deep and meaningful relationships can.

Male and Female

We desperately need to recapture the Genesis portrait of men and women. As we have seen in Genesis 2:18, the man and woman were sexually differentiated and unique, yet they were equal and complementary. The genuine differences between men and women, boys and girls extend far beyond their cultural socialization. The difference is one of nature, not just nurture. We were created for each other, sharing equally in the culture-making mandate of Genesis 1–2. We are to be joined in ways that reflect and even participate in the unity of God. And most importantly, both man and woman are needed to fully reflect the image of God. Certainly, masculinity or femininity alone partially mirrors God's image, but only together do they fully represent Him.

Men and women are equally made in the image of God (Genesis 1:26-27). They share equally in God's blessing, both in their sexuality and creativity and assignment to fill the earth (1:28). Men and women are also equally empowered to have dominion over the created order. Made in the image of God, they are a sign on this planet that this is God's domain and that they serve as vice-regents in His kingdom.

Marriage and Sexuality

Christian marriage finds its basis in Genesis 1–2. To be united, man and woman must first leave father and mother, breaking the old family structure. Their union is to be permanent, not situational or occasional. Second, they are to cleave to each other. The verb is very strong—"united to, laminated together, glued together." Their cleaving is heterosexual; they form a new family unit. Third, they are to become one flesh. Their union is monogamous.

What is this life that man and woman are to live together, naked and unashamed (Genesis 2:25)? They are utterly transparent before each other—no separation. Loneliness is gone. All of this is the intention of the sixth day of creation. God makes us in His image, breathes into us the breath of life, and gives us dominion over the earth. We tend the garden and name the animals. He gives us companionship in the "one flesh" of sexual, permanent, and personal union. There is no warfare between the sexes; they are naked and unashamed.

We were created to reproduce, and fortunately for us, God decided to make that a really enjoyable process. Think about the implications of being naked and unashamed. Adam and Eve had no concept of any other reality than nakedness. And their nakedness simply described their level of intimacy. No shame, no guilt, no barriers, no insecurity, no comparison, no competition. Nothing but joy, delight, intimacy. Why this is so important? It's important because they were sexual before they were sinful. In other words, that part of us that is sexual, including arousal, passion, and release, was part of God's good creation. Our sexuality has been tainted by sin, but being sexual is still a good thing.

The church usually announces precisely the opposite to the world. Sex is bad, shameful, a taboo topic for discussion within the community of followers of Jesus except to remind us to stay away from it. In Genesis 1–2, being sexual is a part of being human, and being human is good. Therefore, being sexual is also good. Far too many of us look at our sexuality as a curse rather than the good gift of a gracious God. God is the author of sex. This isn't the enemy's territory—this is something God ordained for us to enjoy and to knit the hearts and bodies of two people together. This may seem obvious to some of us, but to many others, this is revolutionary and liberating. The point is that sexuality is a wonderful and awesome thing. Our sexuality is woven into the very fabric of our humanness. The church would do well to recognize that whatever we say about sexual ethics to our world must begin with this resounding declaration: *It is good!*

Yet that declaration is tempered in the very first pages of the Bible by the warning of its power. As much as our culture insists otherwise, sexuality isn't simply a function of our body parts. In no other way are two people bonded into one flesh. Deeper than the mere joining of genitals, sex involves the whole person and is the truest joining of bodies, hearts, and souls. The prohibition of sexual activity outside of marriage is based on this profound insight: Intercourse creates this mysterious one-flesh union.

Interestingly, the Hebrew word for intercourse is *to know.* Sex gives us a special kind of knowledge and a new kind of intimacy called "one flesh." Sexuality comes from places deep within us and is the only way we can unite our lives with another. The encounter does something, for better or worse, that cannot be undone. Sex outside of marriage violates the nature of the act itself—it is a life-uniting act without life-uniting commitment. Such sin is not irreversible, but it requires the healing touch of God.

Nothing else that can happen between two human beings has this effect. In no other way can two people experience this kind of oneness. God's gift of sex is good, but it is also powerful. It can be a source of great joy and meaning or a source of great shame and harm. We see that the only thing strong enough to handle its power is marriage: one man, one woman in permanent, monogamous, covenantal relationship.

Sacred and Secular

The opening chapters of Genesis take great pains to distinguish between the Creator and the creation. The two are fundamentally distinct. God is independent, and everything else depends on Him. God is timeless, and the universe began at a moment in time. The created order may declare God's excellence, and as human beings we may reflect God's image, but nothing that has been created is divine.

There is no hint in the creation accounts of a distinction between what is sacred (or religious) and what is secular (or common or not religious). Adam and Eve were invited to be caretakers of the world, ruling *coram deo* (in God's presence). *Culture* is the name we give to organized activities within society, such as making music, government, businesses, and houses. Genesis 1:26-28 is often described as the cultural mandate because human beings are commanded to exercise wise and responsible stewardship over God's world. This means we are to direct creation toward God-honoring ends. It includes exploring and developing what can be achieved in architecture, farming, art, and family life. God has always intended that we should be involved in this kind of work. What we do in this life matters to God; it is not merely training for the life to come.

In Job 38–41, God declares His delight in what He has made. All of creation was designed to declare His excellence. Psalm 24:1 states, "The earth is the LORD's, and everything in it." Creation isn't just about humanity—God's enjoyment of His creation extends to the nonhuman parts as well. The story of creation, fall, redemption, and restoration isn't only a human story; it is also the story of the rest of the world. For instance, in Genesis 9, God makes the rainbow covenant with Noah and every living creature. The biblical drama that starts with creation and ends in *shalom* includes, at each stage, wolves and lambs and all else God has made.

Paul warns about some first-century people who argued against enjoying creation:

> The Spirit clearly says that in later times some will abandon the faith and follow deceiving spirits and things taught by demons. Such teachings come through hypocritical liars, whose consciences have been seared as with a hot iron. They forbid people to marry and order them to abstain from certain foods, which God created to be received with thanksgiving by those who believe and who know the truth. For everything God created is good, and nothing is to be rejected if it is received with thanksgiving, because it is consecrated by the word of God and prayer (1 Timothy 4:1-5).

Creation, even after the fall, is still good. We know this. But beyond knowing it, we must consider its implications. Because we are spiritual beings, we engage in spiritual activities. And here's the point: Human activities are spiritual activities. Eating, drinking, mowing the yard, watching a movie…all of this and more is spiritual because it involves human beings, who are spiritual.

The Value of Human Life

God has ordered His creation. Regardless of the time frame, divine order and the divine purpose stand behind everything. We are not the product of random evolutionary process. Humankind is God's special creation. We have been made in His image. The dignity of our being and identity are grounded in scripture. You will find this nowhere else.

The creation belongs to the Creator, not to us. The days of creation come to a climax in our creation in God's image to reflect His character and do His will on this earth. Every person on the planet today has been made for this same destiny. God has a plan for His universe, this planet, and us, and we are made to participate in it. Our dignity and our destiny are grounded in creation. God gave us the bodies we have. He breathed His life into us, and we live for His purposes. This earth is the arena where we are to live this out. He made it, ordered it, saw that it was good, and blessed it.

Genesis gives us a powerful affirmation of creation, value, meaning, and destiny. This is foundational for our faith. It is foundational to who we are. If this is built into us, it can overcome the tremendous sense of alienation, dislocation, brokenness, fear, and despair that is rampant in our world today. The Bible counters the lies we have believed. Our lives have God-given dignity and meaning and a destiny that includes everything about us. The one who made us and designed us knows what is best for us. If we violate the order of creation, we not only violate the will of God but also step into self-destructive patterns. God not only creates, orders, designs, and purposes this created world but also places us here as part of His creation, with a destiny to live according to and participate in His purposes. God's moral will applies to us.

The creation narrative informs concepts like social justice, mercy, and compassion. With no God and therefore no absolute truth and no transcendent morality, on what basis could we defend the idea of human dignity? The lesson of nature, interpreted through a Darwinian lens, seems to be that the most valuable are the strongest, most cunning, and most worthy of respect. If you want to be treated with human dignity, you must demonstrate that you deserve it. Why should bigotry be wrong if nature values only the beings that prove themselves through strength and cunning?

Ethicist Peter Singer takes the logical implications of a Darwinian worldview to their logical conclusions:

> I have argued that the life of a fetus is of no greater value than the life of a nonhuman animal at a similar level of rationality, self-consciousness, awareness, capacity to feel, etc., and that since no fetus is a person, no fetus has the same claim to life as a person. Now it must be admitted that these arguments apply to the newborn baby as much as to the fetus… If the fetus does not have the same claim to life as a person, it appears that the newborn baby does not either, and the life of a newborn baby is of less value than the life of a pig, a dog, or a chimpanzee.[7]

But here again Genesis paints a subversive picture. From conception, *all* humans are created in God's image. The image of God in humanity is *human as human* (essentially), not merely some element in him or her or a particular manifestation of the image (functionally). Humans *reflect* the image of God in differing degrees and ways, but no one is *created* in the image of God in greater or lesser degrees. Although distorted after the fall, humanity remains created in the image of God (Genesis 9:6; James 3:9). This means that the disabled, the mentally challenged, the elderly, the very young—all whom our society would devalue—are to be nurtured, protected, and fought for. The worth of humans runs far deeper than their ability to function or contribute.

The biblical accounts subvert the narratives of our world in every way possible. From the way we see our world to the way we see ourselves and our relationships with each other, every facet of human existence fits together in God's good design.

The Twisting of
Everything Good

*No one calls on your name
or strives to lay hold of you;
for you have hidden your face from us
and made us waste away because of our sins.*

ISAIAH 64:7

M ost of us would readily acknowledge that our world is deeply broken. Our Internet news sites, our newspapers and magazines, and our television news programming regularly catalog the evils done in our world. We not only hurt each other but also hurt ourselves in endlessly creative ways. Genesis 3–11 explains why this is so. The scriptures don't give us any idea how long the first humans enjoyed life in the garden. What we do know, however, is that after the opening chapters of Genesis provide a breathtaking vision of life under God's rule, we see Adam and Eve choosing to go their own way.

Genesis 3 records what is simply called *the fall.* Though often thought to be myth or legend, this story is put forward as something that actually happened.

Genesis 2 ends with the man and woman in the garden, free to enjoy all it joys and delights, with only the "tree of the knowledge of good and evil" off limits (Genesis 2:17). Why does God issue this command?

Speculations abound regarding the nature of the tree and the knowledge it offers, but at the very least, it reminded Adam and Eve of their limitations as part of God's creation. Though made in God's image, they were not gods themselves and lived under the authority of God in their innocence. They would enjoy the blessings and intimacy of the garden only if they continued to submit to His rule and trust His words to them. Human life has boundaries, and humble obedience is to be our response. But we are free to disobey. The tree of the knowledge of good and evil is a sign of our freedom and responsibility. God includes this element of risk in creation—mankind's freedom to turn from Him—so that we may love Him freely.

In Genesis 3:1, a serpent appears and tempts our first parents (Adam and Eve) into sin. (We read later that the serpent is the vehicle of satanic deception [Revelation 12:9].) The text reveals that our first parents fell with outside help. We know from scripture that Satan came through the serpent to deceive our original parents and bring destruction to the planet. His pride gives birth to their pride. His seduction lures them away from God's kingdom and into his counterfeit kingdom. The tempter appears, and temptation follows.

Notice the sequence of the temptation. First, the serpent questions God: "Did God really say...?" This questioning of God's command and of His goodness leads to doubt about the consequences of disobedience: "You will not surely die." The tempter then offers them an alternative story: "Your eyes will be opened, and you will be like God." First Eve and then Adam listen to Satan's words and chooses to reject God's authority by eating the fruit of this tree. In this decision, Adam and Eve substitute themselves for God and choose independence over dependence, self-will over God-will, their kingdom instead of His kingdom. Adam and Eve sinned by falling for the presumption that they could run their own lives, that they could be like God, that they could live an autonomous existence in this world. Their sin is pride. Pride always separates us from God.

This temptation represents the freedom to be autonomous (from the Greek words *autos* [self] and *nomos* [law]).[1] They can obey God or not; they can submit themselves to Him and experience the *shalom* and blessing of creation, or they can create their own kingdom (the place where their wills are done) and experience death (Genesis 2:17; 3:3). To be autonomous in this sense is to determine for yourself what is right and wrong rather than rely on God's guidance and direction.

The fall itself takes place in verse 6. Adam joins Eve, and the consequences unfold. They do not immediately die, at least not in the physical sense and not right away. But they experience another kind of death as all four dimensions of *shalom* are fractured. They lost their innocence, and the blessedness and unity they shared in their relationships with God, each other, and the world were all distorted. They became aware of their nakedness and hid themselves from each other. They hid from the Lord God in fear and shame, using the very creation (plants and leaves) they were to care for. Their eyes were opened, and rather than becoming like God, they recognized they were naked. Our existence from this point on is shame based. At the end of Genesis 2, we are naked and unashamed. In chapter 3, we are naked, ashamed, hidden, and separated from God and from each other.

Death and sin distort our telos—the way we were made to relate to each other, to God, to ourselves, and to creation. Sin also introduces evil into our world. Evil is not an original part of creation. It is a twisting or distorting of what God made. Evil is rebellion against God and His purposes for creation. This is important to understand because when God makes all things new, He won't destroy creation and begin all over again. Rather, He will destroy the evil that puts His good creation under the "bondage of decay" (Romans 8:21).

Ripples of Corruption

After the fall, the harmony and unity between the sexes ends. The woman's desire for her husband is akin to the desire of sin poised to leap at Cain (Genesis 4:7). Far from being a reign of coequals over the remainder of God's creation, the relationship becomes a fierce dispute as each party tries to rule the other. The two who once reigned as one attempt to rule each other.

Notice how the effects of Adam and Eve's rebellion begin to spread through all of creation. They notice they are naked, and then they hide from each other and from God. In chapter 3, God comes looking for Adam and Eve and asks them how they discovered their nakedness. Adam blames the woman, and the woman blames the serpent.

Sin begins to infect every part of human life. God curses the serpent, so conflict enters into a creation once marked by perfect *shalom*. God then judges the woman and the man.

The judgment on the woman affects her sexuality and her connection with the man. The domination of the male over the female is part of God's judgment on the race after the fall and not a part of His divine order in creation. In this context the fact that one shall rule over the other is not an imperative order of creation but rather a result of the broken connection between God, the man, and the woman. It brings disorder, which disturbs the original peace of creation. The relationship between the man and woman becomes one of self-serving mastery rather than selfless love (Genesis 3:16).

Woman moves from being coequal in dominion to being dominated by her relational desire. She moves out of the covenant relationship with God and into self-rule or living under the man's rule. Reproduction was a central aspect of the woman's original caretaking and dominion. Had sin not entered the world, this would have been a wholly joyful and satisfying experience. But now this is frustrated not only by her physical pain but also by the disruption of her intimacy with the man. God warns the woman that she will experience an unreciprocated longing for intimacy with the man. Neither childbearing nor intimacy with man will provide the kind of satisfaction and completion she longs for. She will have an unsatisfied hunger and thirst that no human relationship can fill.

The judgment on the man in Genesis 3:17-19 is a cursed ground, hard work, toil, opposition, struggle, thorns and thistles, sweat, exhaustion, and death. Man moves from exercising dominion to exercising domination from being a steward of God's world to trying to own it, from covenant relationship to self-rule. The man and woman were once with God, in God's place, under God's rule. But now they are separated from God, in their own place, under the man's rule.

In his sinful and fallen state, the man abuses the power and authority given to both man and woman. Now he seeks to dominate the bone of his bone and flesh of his flesh. He actively and passively dominates everything to scratch fruit from the earth, to meet personal agendas of achievement, to make a name for himself. He selfishly dominates at the expense of his calling—oneness and unity of purpose with God and the woman. Regardless of how clever man is, how hard he works or doesn't work, or how much pleasure or wealth he accumulates, he is never satisfied. God allowed sin its consequences, knowing that it would ensure humanity's dissatisfaction.

With these judgments, Adam and Eve are expelled from Eden. An angelic guard is set. Their access to the tree of life is eliminated until Jesus returns.

Cain and Abel

The stain of sin and death continue to spread outward. As the children were born to the first family, the pattern of sin and corruption that began with the fall continue. Anger and jealously lead to the first murder as Cain kills his younger brother Abel. This is the first death recorded in the scriptures. Adam and Eve's sin manifests itself in their offspring. As their family continues to grow, two distinct lines of moral descent emerge: those who follow after Cain and share in his rebellion against God, and those who follow after Abel and approach God with trust and obedience.

Cain marries, and his wife gives birth to a son named Enoch. Cain decides to build a city and name it after his son. Cain and his tribe are still made in the image of God, but now they (we) have a terrible capacity to use for evil the wonderful things God has created for good.

God's gracious gifts (family life, worship, provision, and the like) can be turned into sources of strife and conflict. Expressions of the cultural mandate abound as people develop new cultural practices and forms (Genesis 4:17-22), but they can be misdirected and twisted. Lamech twists God's design for marriage by marrying two women, and he uses poetry, which is part of the good enterprise of culture making, to celebrate murder and revenge. Metalworking, agriculture, and music also emerge, but even these things eventually become twisted by fallen humanity.

Noah and the Flood

After Abel, Eve gave birth to another son, Seth, and he continued the line of Abel. Both the line of Cain and the line of Seth were active on the earth, but humanity as a whole became more and more evil. Eventually the only man who walked with God was Noah (from the line of Abel and Seth). God was about to judge sin, but He gave grace to one man, and through this one man, a family was saved (Genesis 6–9).

The "sons of God" appear in 6:2,4. Who are they? Most certainly, they are demons. Job 1:6; 2:1; and 38:7 refer to them as angels (the NASB uses the more literal translation "sons of God"). Psalm 89:6 refers to them as heavenly beings (or "sons of the mighty" in the NASB). But these angelic beings invade earth and increase the volume and depth of human rebellion and depravity. A theme of deeper and darker evil rippling outward continues after the fall. The wickedness on the earth becomes so great that God regrets creating human beings and determines to cleanse the earth of them. Evil is universal, so the catastrophic judgment is a universal flood—an uncreation. Massive amounts of water are unleashed on the earth. The judgment is terrible, but God's gracious commitment to His original purposes for humanity remain intact.[2]

Two themes run in opposition. First is the theme of cataclysm, sin, rebellion, devastation, demonic activity, and human pride and presumption. Then comes the theme of Noah's righteousness. God calls Noah and reveals His purpose to him. Noah's task is to save his family and representative animals from disaster. The growing infection of sin and evil brings us to another crisis point in Genesis 6. Noah is a type of Adam—he is commissioned in the same way Adam was. (Compare Genesis 1:28 with 9:1,7.) Only his family and the animals are saved from the flood. A new beginning for the human race parallels the original beginning in Adam.

In chapter 9, God makes a covenant with Noah (and with us) to never again destroy all life with a flood. The rainbow is a sign of His promise. He sets a boundary for people shedding other people's blood (9:5-6). This is the beginning of some primitive governmental structure for human life. There is the blessing to be fruitful and multiply and the divine covenant not to destroy the world again by water. This covenant reflects the unconditional and perpetual "royal grant" that a king gives to one who has served him, and it reminds us that God is King, ruling from His throne. As the mighty King, He then makes a covenant with those who serve Him. This is a sign of His grace. He continues to sustain the earth, even though sin and corruption will spread once again. The corruption of the human heart remains (6:5; 8:21). The whole of the earth descends from Noah and his family—Shem, Ham, Japheth—but sin soon shows itself again in Noah's family (9:20-28). Culture advances, but not always in ways that honor God. Noah is the first to plant a vine and make wine, but he gets drunk and disgraces himself and his family.

Tower of Babel

After the flood, Noah's sons begin the repopulation of the earth. God repeats the cultural mandate with Noah (9:7). Noah's descendants increase but stay localized, rather than fill the earth. They had one language and settled on a plain (Genesis 11:1-9).

But even after a fresh start, humanity was incapable of following God's ways. People's hearts were bent on reputation, glory, fame, renown, achievement—all apart from God. "Let us build ourselves a city, with a tower that reaches to the heavens, so that we may make a name for ourselves and not be scattered over the face of the whole earth." The impulse to build a city is part of normal cultural development within God's world. But this can be misdirected, and as people migrate eastward, they build a city with a huge tower. This is their way of asserting their own will against God's desire that mankind should spread out and "fill the earth."

These pioneers build a tower to reach into heaven, one of the large artificial mountains (ziggurats) excavated in Ur and elsewhere. They were topped with temples. These sacred mountains, in a sense, reached to the heavens. The people built the tower to secure themselves ("make a name for ourselves"), to find permanence in their own religious and spiritual inventions, or idols. God views this as a seeking for power (11:6).

This appears to be a repetition of the eating from the tree of the knowledge of good and evil but now performed on a grand social scale. By building this tower, they arrogantly challenge God to come down and bless their endeavor. In 11:5-6, God does come down (ironically, because the tower is not big enough to be seen), and far from blessing the project, God condemns the arrogance that inspired it. He judges the people by confusing their language and scattering them abroad.

Babel stands as a monument to the perennial human desire to build our own kingdom apart from God. Judgment, though, is always accompanied by mercy, and Genesis 12 marks an entirely new chapter in the outworking of God's telos for creation.

As Genesis opens, the earth is the place where God's will is done. He simply speaks, and creation obeys. But by the end of Genesis 11, the earth has become the place where *other* wills are done also. As the psalmist declares, "The highest heavens belong to the LORD, but the earth he has given to man" (Psalm 115:16). The difference between the heavens and the earth is now clearly marked. This will cause Jesus to teach His disciples to pray, "Your kingdom come, your will be done on earth as it is in heaven" (Matthew 6:10). Genesis 3–11 shows us how dark the world has become as a result of sin. Cornelius Plantinga aptly summarizes the nature and effects of sin:

> Sin is the missing of a target, a wandering from the path, a straying from the fold. Sin is a hard heart and a stiff neck. Sin is blindness and deafness. It is both the overstepping of a line and the failure to reach it—both transgression and shortcoming... Sin is disruption of created harmony and resistance to divine restoration of that harmony.[3]

Glimpses of Redemption

God does not give up on His purposes for His creation and kingdom. Though Adam and Eve flee, God pursues. Though they are exposed and naked, He clothes them.[4] Though judged and driven from the garden, God promises to provide help (3:15): The woman's offspring will be at war with the serpent and will ultimately crush his head. God promises to destroy the forces of darkness that Adam and Eve unleashed. This is the first promise of redemption—Christ is the seed of the woman, and He will defeat Satan, though at great cost to Himself (His heel will be wounded).

The flood shows God to be a holy Judge and gracious Redeemer. After the flood is over, God makes a covenant, or agreement, with His people that ties the two together, though not as equal partners. God is making a new start with Noah, but His purposes for creation are the same. The content of the covenant with Noah extends to all of creation.

God still protects His creation. He covers Adam and Eve, marks Cain, and saves righteous Noah and his family along with the animals from the flood. All of this anticipates God's call to Abram and His intervention to bless him and begin reversing the curse of the fall.

Echoes and Ashes:
The Vandalism of *Shalom*

Sin...becomes the punishment of sin.

ST. AUGUSTINE

Sin does not build shalom; it vandalizes it.

CORNELIUS PLANTINGA

Like the story of creation in Genesis 1–2, the story of the fall in chapters 3–11 is quite subversive of many of our modern narratives. We reflect the same hubris that built the tower of Babel as we continue to seek mastery of our world through science and technology, regardless of consequence. We may boast of our ability to cure disease, map the human genome, or choose the gender of our children, but despite the many good things brought about by medicine, physics, and biology, we are still unable to remove the stain of sin in us and in our world. Malcom Muggeridge laments our current situation:

> It has become abundantly clear in the second half of the twentieth century that Western Man has decided to abolish himself. Having wearied of the struggle to be himself, he has created his own boredom out of his own affluence, his own impotence out of his own erotomania, his own

vulnerability out of his own strength; himself blowing the trumpet that brings the walls of his own city tumbling down, and, in a process of auto-genocide, convincing himself that he is too numerous, and labouring accordingly with pill and scalpel and syringe to make himself fewer in order to be an easier prey for his enemies; until at last, having educated himself into imbecility, and polluted and drugged himself into stupefaction, he keels over a weary, battered old brontosaurus and becomes extinct.[1]

The steady upward progress and "evolution" of humanity is a modern myth flatly contradicted by the fall. Yes, much of our cultural work is beneficial, but it can also be twisted in ways that distort God's design beyond recognition. The same medicine and technology that leads to innovative cures also engineers biological weapons. The same physics that sends us into space also designs nuclear weaponry. What was true of the earliest humans is true of us today.

This is offensive to modern ears. The presence of sin, death, and evil strike against the human presumption of progress. Regardless of our technology, our advances in health care, and our ability to subdue creation around us, we will still die. Good, created things will still be used for evil. New illnesses will need diagnoses and cure. Human nature will find new ways to self-destruct. Even with our progress, we are still born ashamed, lonely, empty, and fundamentally alienated from God and from each other.

The feelings of shame are passed down and reinforced through the generations. Each of us comes to know that something is fundamentally wrong with *us* and not merely with our behavior or thoughts. Shame is one of the central features of human existence after the fall. All of this alienation and separation implants the consequences of the fall deep within our very being. We become ashamed of shame and build a wall of anger around it. Our abandonment of God, starting in Eden, results in our separation and alienation from Him. This creates a deep sense of shame, which is the source of the "hole in the soul," that inner anxiety that the core of our being is empty. Nothing is there.

Our response, modeled on Adam and Eve, is to cover up. We fear exposure, and we fear facing the results of abandonment, depression, aching loneliness, and the loss of our true self. In the place of God's image in us, we create the false self, the public mask that we hide behind. Having disconnected themselves from God and the *shalom* of obeying His word, humanity looks to creation as a cure for shame (Genesis 3:7). They used leaves from a fig tree to cover up their sexual differences, thereby hiding the core of who they are from each other. But creation is not the cure for their shame. Neither is relationship, work (dominion), or anything else in creation.

We are made in God's image, but we can say no to Him. In the fall, humanity says no to the boundaries that God has established for us. We fall every day when we say no to those boundaries. God's desire for us is to be naked and unashamed before Him and before each other. But we are not, so we cover up. So much of the brokenness that Jesus came to redeem and heal and to restore us from is that cover-up and isolation, that deep and shame-based loneliness. We need a new creation. We need to be born again. The old creation now stands under a curse—the infection of sin and the judgment of God. As the Bible narrates the fall from Eden, it guides us to a course correction, as Cornelius Plantinga suggests:

> The big systemic evils exasperate us. So many of them seem beyond human reach. They partake of the mystery of iniquity. But then, so do our personal sins. Why would we and others live against God, who is our highest good, the source of our very lives? Why do we human beings live against each other, fighting over cultural differences instead of enjoying them, envying each other's gifts instead of celebrating them? Why would we human creatures live against the rest

of creation, given its majesty and abundance? Why would we live against the purpose of our own existence?[2]

The Breadth and Depth of Sin and Fallenness

As we have seen, sin and its effects begin with Adam and Eve and ripple outward. Sin and evil are not simply the absence of good or the result of a mistaken choice. As Robert Webber says, "Evil is revolt, disobedience, resistance. It is a human (and demonic) refusal to carry out God's purposes in history. It is deliberate, intentional, and violent rejection of God."[3] Sin is dynamic and reproductive: It gives birth to more of itself. Sin begets sin. It is relentless and corrosive. In our world, nothing that is pure will stay that way. Even reformers need constant reforming, revolutionaries will need revolution, and rescuers will need rescue. Plantinga puts it concisely: "Evil contaminates every scalpel designed to remove it."[4]

How Far Down the Darkness Goes

So we may speak of the scope of sin both in terms of its breadth and its depth. When I say sin has depth, I mean that it strikes at the very core of who we are. It doesn't exist only on the surface of human existence, but comes from the heart:

> Again Jesus called the crowd to him and said, "Listen to me, everyone, and understand this. Nothing outside a man can make him 'unclean' by going into him. Rather, it is what comes out of a man that makes him 'unclean.'"
>
> After he had left the crowd and entered the house, his disciples asked him about this parable. "Are you so dull?" he asked. "Don't you see that nothing that enters a man from the outside can make him 'unclean'? For it doesn't go into his heart but into his stomach, and then out of his body." (In saying this, Jesus declared all foods "clean.")
>
> He went on: "What comes out of a man is what makes

him 'unclean.' For from within, out of men's hearts, come evil thoughts, sexual immorality, theft, murder, adultery, greed, malice, deceit, lewdness, envy, slander, arrogance and folly. All these evils come from inside and make a man 'unclean'" (Mark 7:14-23).

Adam and Eve passed their original sin to their children, and it became generational sin. Cain did not sin because he woke up one day and decided to sin. It was already in his heart. What happened in the exchange between himself and his brother brought out what was implicitly there. How did it get there? In part, because of what Adam and Eve did in the garden. We will never understand the depth of our condition and the depth of God's answer in Jesus Christ apart from understanding original sin. A generational infection is carried down to us. This explains the sad, violent, brutal history of the human race. Paul says that sin abounds; it accumulates and gathers momentum. Sin is rebellion, a violation of God's will. It is a surrender to satanic seduction, lies, and deception. It is pride and vanity. It is recognizing other gods and putting them before God.

The critical issue is not the act of sinning but rather the heart attitude behind the act. The moment we enthrone ourselves and call ourselves god, we receive the bitter consequences of our rebellion and pass them on. Abel's blood cries out from the ground because of what Adam and Eve did in the garden. Sin grows quantitatively throughout the generations. It includes not only human pride and rebellion but also demonic interference. This combination brings us to catastrophic evil and catastrophic judgment.

Genesis 1–2 shows that human existence was to be centered in and oriented around God.[5] This means that we are fundamentally religious. By *religious* I don't mean that human beings are always looking for rules to live by or rituals to perform to please angry gods. No, I mean that we were built to worship—driven to find an object (something or someone) to bow down to. We need to orient our lives around something. This understanding of worship (the ascribing of worth to something) shows that it is a human activity, not just the province of choirs or hymnals, but of everybody. Atheists, Hindus, Wiccans, skeptics…anyone and everyone on the face of the earth is a worshipper. We can't help ourselves. An essential part of our humanness is the need to orient our lives around something.

When people are alienated and separated from God, they do not stop worshipping (being religious); rather, they give their worship to something or someone else. But this exposes the extent of sin in our hearts. We are bent so that we would prefer to worship the creation and not the Creator. We must give our religious allegiance to something, and idolatry, at its core, is the substitution of the worship of an idol for the worship of the one true God. Paul puts it like this: "They exchanged the truth of God for a lie, and worshiped and served created things rather than the Creator—who is forever praised. Amen" (Romans 1:25). Sin is not only a trespass or violation of God's will but also a transfer of something God justly deserves (our respect, honor, worship) to a lesser object.

The Pervasiveness of Sin

When I speak of sin's breadth, I mean that sin and its effects touch every aspect of human life and of the creation. The human family and all of creation are corrupt in every aspect. Sin is pervasive, and every part of human nature is distorted. No part of a human being or creation is untouched by sin and evil. No part of our humanity is as bad as it could be, yet neither is any part as good as it could be. We are subject to illness, disease, and death; we use imagination and reason to justify and rationalize our sin and rebellion. We are guilty before God and alienated from Him. We are called to care for our world, yet we are more often frustrated by it. Everything we touch is subject to decay.

Sin did not destroy the image of God in humankind; even in our fallen, broken state we reflect God in a manner that nothing else does.

Nor has the fall abrogated the cultural mandate; in fact, after the flood, God repeats it to Noah (Genesis 9:1-7). God's intention for people to build an earthly culture for His glory is now corrupted by our attempts to build an earthly culture for our own glory (like the tower of Babel), but nevertheless, the mandate itself remains intact.

But the creation itself now works against us. Death, decay, and corruption have also spread to nonhuman creation, so Paul says creation was "subjected to frustration, not by its own choice, but by the will of the one who subjected it… The whole creation has been groaning as in the pains of childbirth right up to the present time" (Romans 8:20,22). Though the fall has not pushed out all the goodness, order, and purpose from God's creation, all of those things—human and nonhuman alike—now sit under the weight of human sin and await redemption and restoration.

Another way to measure the depth and breadth of sin is to note the price God paid to atone for it: the giving and suffering of His only Son, Jesus, to defeat sin and its consequences. This tells us that what is wrong with the world is desperately difficult to fix, and that its repair required God's direct, supernatural, and sacrificial intervention.

The Origins of Evil

One of the most pressing questions people ask about God is how to reconcile His nature (all-knowing, all-powerful, all-good) with the reality of evil and suffering in the world. Many shake their fists at God and wonder why He allows evil in the world if He has the power to stop it. Genesis 3–11 helps us answer that question: God's will is not the only will at work in the universe.

In Genesis 2, the man and woman are given a straightforward command: Do not eat from the tree of the knowledge of good and evil. They choose to disobey. Sin and its consequences are revealed: separation from God, the distortion of nature, the violation of human life, demonic activity. Genesis 6 reveals the demonic world. Without much background, we find that some angels, like the humans, have chosen to rebel against God's rule over them. They work against God by working against His creation. We learn more about these fallen angels in later parts of the scripture, but Genesis 6 clearly intends to show us that they harm humanity and work against God's purposes on the earth.

This doesn't answer all our questions, but it is a start. We can answer that evil things happen on the earth because fallen angels and fallen humans exercise some degree of choice. Even so-called natural evils, such as earthquakes, tornados, and floods, are results of human and demonic sin. All of creation now groans under the reality of sin, death, and corruption.

The Need for Rescue

So both the breadth and depth of sin in this world and the reality of the demonic help us make sense of the world we find ourselves in. We can choose to pretend that we are basically good people who occasionally make mistakes (usually because of our genetics, a physical weakness, or the way we were raised). Or we can believe the biblical story, which portrays a different picture. Creation is still good, and humanity still bears the unmistakable imprint of God (sin hasn't completely pushed out either of those), but the fall forces us to concede that the solution to human life and human problems lies beyond humanity itself.

Our natural inclination, regardless of whether we are religious—is to work at it ourselves, try harder, and find a way to make ourselves right before God. I have many friends and family who simply declare, "If God won't let someone like me into heaven, I don't want to be there." Others place their faith in their own adherence to religious systems or principles. But ultimately, all religious systems—Eastern, Western, and everything in between—focus on being good (though they their definitions of *being good* differ).[6]

That is the subversive nature of Genesis 3–11. It requires us to admit that we need help, that we need to be rescued, that our best efforts don't address the real problems in humanity and the world. Education, government, relationships, money, pleasure...all these things can help but don't solve the fundamental problem. Genesis 1–11 announces that we were made for God and by God and that we are now born into a state of alienation from God. Our hope, therefore, must come from outside ourselves, though our sin makes us loath to admit it. Even with all our knowledge, technology, and sophistication, we are still in the same situation as the prophet:

> So justice is far from us,
>   and righteousness does not reach us.
> We look for light, but all is darkness;
>   for brightness, but we walk in deep shadows.
> Like the blind we grope along the wall,
>   feeling our way like men without eyes.
> At midday we stumble as if it were twilight;
>   among the strong, we are like the dead (Isaiah 59:9-10).

The Cosmic Rescue Operation

*We tell the story of a God who...completes what he
has begun, a God who comes to the rescue of those who
seem lost and enslaved in the world the way it now is.*

N.T. WRIGHT

The major theme in Genesis 3–11 is sin and judgment, but the overall sense is that God has a purpose and a plan beyond this. In His original design, His creation lives in harmony and fellowship with Him under His blessing, reflecting His image, and doing His will. Creation was to be the sign that He is the only Lord and we are the sole agents of His dominion. The end of the story assures us that Satan cannot thwart this plan by demons, by human rebellion, or by all the generational consequences of the fall (Revelation 20:10 and chapters 21–22).

We see that sin is not natural to this world or to us; it entered the world, so it must be able to be removed from the world. We also see God working to restrain evil in Genesis 3–11. He speaks, moves, judges, and shows mercy. He has not remained distant from our world—far from it! He has entered into human history to work, rescue, and restore.

God's work in our world for the purposes of restoration is often called *redemptive history*. It implies three characteristics about God's saving work that will be demonstrated in this chapter and those that follow. Goheen and Bartholomew refer to this:

First, salvation is progressive: God's redemptive work commences near the dawn of human history, and we have not reached sunset yet. Second, salvation is restorative: God's saving work is about reclaiming His lost creation, putting it back to the way it was meant to be. Third, salvation is comprehensive: all of human life and all of the nonhuman creation are the object of God's restorative work.[1]

Redemptive history is simply the record of God's work to bring about the salvation of those who call on Christ and the renewal of the heavens and the earth, cleansing it from the stain of sin and death. All of this is done through Jesus Christ, but it unfolds in three stages (we are living in the last stage).

The Formation of Israel

Call

In response to the fall and the catastrophes of the flood and the tower of Babel, God begins to redeem His creation by calling one man, Abram (who we know is later renamed Abraham). He asks Abraham to leave his home and family and follow God wherever He leads. Abraham obeys, displaying a faith and trust in God that is the opposite of what we saw at Babel. That tower was supposed to bring reputation, security, blessing, community...things that God freely gives to Abraham. God's response to the fall was to call one man and build his descendants into a nation that would bring blessing to the whole world (Genesis 18:18-19).

God makes a covenant with Abraham that includes these blessings, promising that nothing will frustrate His purposes. Indeed, God overcomes many different obstacles—including infertility, old age, famine, human stupidity and sinfulness—and remains faithful to the promises He made to Abraham (see, for example, 45:5-7; 50:20). God gives the covenant and its promises as part of His plan to bless the nations. The rest of the Old Testament chronicles the gradual unfolding and partial fulfillment of God's promises to Abraham and the formation of God's people from Abraham's offspring.

Abraham has amazing faith, but Genesis candidly shows that even he is imperfect and sinful (he doubts God and lies about his wife). His sin is passed along to his descendants, including Isaac, Jacob and Esau, and Joseph and his brothers. The Bible records their actions and attitudes with unflinching honesty, not to condone such sinfulness, but to show how God works through such people to bring about His purposes. Even when Israel becomes part of the problem and ends up needing rescue, God's purposes remain steadfast.

Covenant

Roughly 400 years after the end of Genesis, Israel is in Egypt, enslaved to an oppressive pharaoh (Psalm 105:42-43). But ironically, God uses Pharaoh to orchestrate Israel's escape from captivity (Exodus 9:16).

God again decides to use one man as His instrument of blessing. He calls Moses to be the means of the nation's deliverance from Egypt. Through a series of miraculous signs and wonders (plagues that each target a specific Egyptian god), God rescues His people from their slavery and oppression to Pharaoh.[2] The moment of deliverance comes on the night of the tenth plague, in which God destroys the Egyptians' firstborn male children and animals but "passes over" the Israelites (Exodus 12). This event becomes the basis of the annual celebration of Passover, in which Israel will remember God's great act of deliverance for generations to come. The entire exodus event profoundly shapes the memory and narrative theology of the Israelites. They come to know God first as Rescuer and Redeemer, and only afterward do they discover that God made the universe and everything in it.

Three months after the exodus, God leads Israel to Mt. Sinai. There He reveals His purposes for them. He has chosen them in an act of grace and mercy (Exodus 19:3-6; Deuteronomy 7:7-8) to be His treasured possession out of all the nations of the world (Exodus 19:5-6). But

God's choice of Israel is not just for their sake; it is also for the sake of the nations. Israel is to be different from the other nations. They are to be holy, reflecting God's character through the way they live and functioning as a kingdom of priests to the people of the world. Israel is to be a model people, called out from the nations for the sake of the nations to be a light to the nations. In every dimension of their lives, they are to be the vehicle and paradigm of God's redemption. Israel's life and obedience to God showcases what He intends for the nations of the world.

God introduces a new covenant to formalize Israel's mission as God's people in relationship with Him (Exodus 19–24). This covenant matches the style of other treaties of that time between kings and their subjects. God gives the Ten Commandments to Israel (Exodus 20; Deuteronomy 5) as the broad conditions or terms of the covenant. They reflect God's purposes for humanity and show Israel how to live in ways that mirror God's character. The law or instructions that follow the Ten Commandments develop detailed applications of the commandments in a multitude of situations.

God then instructs Israel to build a tabernacle to house His presence among them and centralize their formal worship. Sacrifice is necessary for sinners to come into God's presence, and the Levities are chosen to administer various offerings and sacrifices. As Exodus ends, God fills the tabernacle with His presence and dwells there (Exodus 40:34-38). God permanently lives with His people, foreshadowing the restoration of God's presence in all of creation.

> At this small, lonely place in the midst of the chaos of the wilderness, a new creation comes into being. In the midst of disorder there is order. The tabernacle is the world order as God intended writ small in Israel. The priests of the sanctuary going about their appointed courses is like everything in creation performing its liturgical service—the sun, the trees, human beings. The people of Israel carefully encamped around the tabernacle in their midst constitutes

the beginnings of God's bringing creation back to what it was originally intended to be. The tabernacle is a realization of God's created order in history; both reflect the glory of God in their midst.

Moreover, this microcosm of creation is the beginning of a macrocosmic effort on God's part. In and through His people, God is on the move to a new creation for all. God's presence in the tabernacle is a statement about God's intended presence throughout the entire world. The glory manifest there is to stream out into the larger world. The shining of Moses' face in the wake of the experience of divine glory... is to become characteristic of Israel as a whole, a radiating out into the larger world of those glorious effects of God's dwelling among Israel. As a kingdom of priests...they have a role of mediating this glory to the entire cosmos.[3]

Kingdom

The book of Numbers recounts the journey from Sinai to the Promised Land, which is fraught with rebellion and judgment, grace and mercy. In the book of Joshua, the second generation of Israelites arrives into the Promised Land and, with God's help, proceeds to displace the nations there. The book of Judges catalogs Israel's continued failure to be a light to the nations. The continuing cycle of Israel's disobedience, God's covenant judgment, Israel's repentance, and God's deliverance leads the nation to desire their own a king. Samuel, the last and greatest of the judges, is chosen to be kingmaker.

Monarchy for Israel is very much a mixed bag.[4] Saul's sin and rebellion leads to David's kingship, the standard by which all other kings will be measured. Solomon's early reign is glorious; Israel builds the temple and God's presence fills it, and the nations hear about Israel's reputation and the wonders God has done. But even this leads to the division of the one nation into two warring factions: the northern and southern kingdoms, Israel and Judah. Centuries of idolatry, rebellion, and apostasy follow and lead to exile—the ultimate expression of the failure of God's chosen people to live as a light into the nations. They are scattered across the known world.

Years later, some return to rebuild the temple and the city of Jerusalem, but many remain in exile. The Old Testament closes with Israel back in the Promised Land but without its former glory and the visible manifestation of God's presence. Therefore, they long for the coming of God's Messiah (the anointed King from the line of David) to end exile and fulfill all the promises that had been given to Abraham, Jacob, Moses, and David.[5]

The Coming of Jesus

God reigns sovereignly over human history, so even with all this uncertainty, His purposes will triumph. In the midst of exile, Jeremiah speaks of a new covenant (Jeremiah 31) and Ezekiel speaks of a new temple (Ezekiel 40–48). Isaiah prophesies the advent of a suffering servant who will truly be a light to the nations (Isaiah 49:6; 52:13–53:12).

These images describe a time when God will act decisively to restore His rule on the earth and His people over the nations. The Messiah, the anointed King, will come, and Israel will turn to God once more (Micah 5:1-5; Malachi 3–4). Through the restored Israel, God will bring salvation and redemption to the Gentiles throughout the world and ultimately to the whole earth itself. This will happen in the last chapter of human history, when God's Spirit is poured out on His people and the knowledge of God fills the earth. This present age will close when God acts in power to rescue all things from the ravages of sin, death, and corruption and restores His good rule over the earth.

The best way for the prophets to inspire the people to cling to these hopes and visions was by helping them to envision the wonderful kingdom of God. Israel yearned for the day when all will be put back to the way God intended. The temple will be cleansed, the land will be purified, and God will dwell again with His people (Malachi 3:1). He will deliver the nation from the oppression of foreign rulers in the same way He delivered it from Egypt and Babylon centuries before.

Jesus of Nazareth revealed the kingdom of God in a new way. In Him, the power of God was present to cast out demons, to heal, and to renew. Jesus shows us that God's future salvation includes freedom from the pain and death that we continue to experience in this life and also from the powers of evil and corruption that currently run the world. In His death and resurrection, Jesus inaugurates the new world that the Old Testament prophets envisioned. He declares that the power of the old age has passed away and the new age has dawned in and through Him. Jesus is the climax of the long story of Israel: He was faithful where Israel failed and was steadfast where Israel fell into sin. We cannot understand Jesus' significance apart from that framework.

The gospels (Matthew, Mark, Luke, and John) tell the story of Jesus Himself, the climax of the story of Israel and the fulfillment of the promises of God given to Abraham, Isaac, and Jacob.

The theme of Jesus' entire mission is the kingdom of God (Mark 1:14-15). Jesus announces that God's kingdom has come at last to Israel, and it has done so in Him (Luke 4:18-21). The Father sent Him to preach the good news of the kingdom (Luke 4:43)—that God, through Jesus of Nazareth, is restoring His rightful governance over all humanity and all creation. Jesus gathers a small community of disciples who take up His call to repent, believe, and follow Him (Mark 1:15-20).

As Jesus begins His public ministry, His claim to be God's Messiah is validated through signs and wonders that reveal God's power at work in Him (Mark 1:21-45). These miracles provide a foretaste of what God intends for all humanity. [6]

Opposition to Jesus grows as He and the religious leaders clash over various traditional Jewish practices (Mark 2:1–3:6; Luke 5:17–6:11). Jesus challenges the status quo of the religious elite, announcing and embodying a view of the kingdom of God that was radically new and different from what the reigning guardians of Jewish culture and religion were looking for. Jesus forgives sins outside the temple and on His own authority (Mark 2:1-12), and He begins to share meals with outcasts, sinners, and the unclean. Jesus accuses the religious leaders of forsaking Israel's true identity and calling as a missionary people, and His actions and words present a vision of what Israel was always meant to be.

Many people expected God's Messiah to achieve a decisive and final military victory over those who oppress Israel and oppose God. But Jesus announces that this is not the battle for which He is preparing. He tells His followers that He must suffer and die, taking the full force of Satan and evil upon Himself in order to drain its power. He will conquer evil by allowing it to conquer Him; His death will bring many life. He wins, not through violence, but by giving up His own life on the cross. However, neither the disciples nor the crowds understand the true nature of Jesus' kingship and kingdom.

Jesus' view of His mission is dramatically portrayed in the Last Supper (Mark 14:12-16). This was the annual Passover meal that celebrated Israel's redemption from Egypt during Moses' time (Exodus 12). By Jesus' day, Passover also symbolized Jewish hope for a new exodus, the coming of the kingdom of God, and the establishment of a new covenant that would lead to their complete return from exile. Jesus infused the Passover meal with new meaning (Mark 14:22-25). He announced that His death will usher in the new covenant and the forgiveness of sins.

After a pretense of a trial, Jesus' crucifixion and resurrection represent the culmination of the long story of redemption. Everything in the story of Israel pointed to Jesus and His work. And the ramifications of both these events extend far beyond validating that Jesus is the Messiah. Through Jesus, God accomplishes salvation for individuals and for the entire creation. The cross is central to God's work of redemption. The gospels devote enormous space to the crucifixion accounts, and the letters of the New Testament interpret its significance in various ways. In some places, Jesus' death and resurrection represent God's victory over Satan in the cosmic war that has engulfed the world. Other places indicate that Jesus fulfilled the Old Testament sacrificial system by being the innocent, unblemished sacrifice who took the place of the guilty so that covenant relationship may be restored. Jesus is also our representative, a second Adam, to use Paul's phrase. Through faith in Jesus, we can share in His life, death, and resurrection (Romans 6).

The cross and empty tomb are all these things and more. They are the ultimate victory of the kingdom of God over the kingdoms of the world that are contrary to God's rule. God's perfect reign in creation was disrupted by human rebellion and all that came with it—demonic power, sickness, suffering, pain, death...every kind of evil. The root of all opposition to God's rule was human rebellion, and that could be destroyed only on the cross.

The New Testament writers grapple with how to make sense of these completely unexpected events. Jesus' resurrection has implications beyond His own return to life (John 11). He acts on behalf of all of us and the whole creation. In dying, He takes upon Himself the judgment of the world; in rising, He inaugurates the renewal of the whole creation, including the physical bodies of men and women who are in Christ. Jesus' resurrection is a foreshadowing of our own: He is the firstborn in all creation. That is, He is the first person to rise into God's new world (Colossians 1:15,18; Revelation 1:5), the first-fruits of the resurrection (1 Corinthians 15:20,23), and the author of our salvation (Hebrews 2:10). We can enter that kingdom as we follow Him—enter in foretaste on this side of the consummated kingdom and enter fully on the renewed earth.

The Birth of the Church

The goal of God's redemptive work is to restore His creation from the effects of sin. In His death, Jesus conquered sin, and in His resurrection He has inaugurated a new era of salvation and restoration. This in-between time, after Jesus' first coming and before He comes again, is the time for God's people, empowered by God's Spirit, to continue Jesus' work on the earth.

Jesus commissioned His disciples to continue the work He began (Matthew 28:18) by baptizing new disciples into the community of the church and teaching them the way of Jesus. Jesus said, "As the Father has sent me, I am sending you" (John 20:21). The newly gathered community is to carry out its mission in the same way Jesus carried out His mission. It is to announce the good news of the kingdom of God, which includes forgiveness of sins (John 20:23), and to witness to what they have seen and heard from Jesus (Luke 24:46-49; Acts 1:8). Jesus breathed the Holy Spirit into His disciples shortly after His resurrection (John 20:22; also see Genesis 2:7; Ezekiel 37:5-10) and poured out the Spirit on them again on Pentecost (Acts 2:1-4). Only through the Holy Spirit can the church carry out its mission.

The book of Acts is a companion volume to Luke's gospel and tells the story of the continuing work of Jesus after His return to His Father. He works through His Spirit and His church to bring salvation to the world. During His earthly ministry, Jesus primarily confined His work to Israel, but after Pentecost, His work began to fill the earth (Acts 1:8).

The Old Testament had promised that in the last days the Holy Spirit would be given to the Messiah (Isaiah 42:1), Israel (Ezekiel 37:14), and the nations (Joel 2:28-32). After His resurrection, Jesus promised that the Holy Spirit would be poured out on His disciples (Acts 1:4-5). This happens a few days after Jesus' ascension, during the feast of Pentecost. Peter explains that this is the fulfillment of Joel's prophecy that the Holy Spirit would be poured out in the last days (Acts 2:14-36). These days have come, ushered in by the life, death, and resurrection of Jesus. The disciples witnessed these things, and Jesus commanded them to carry their testimony to the world.

The Holy Spirit becomes the primary personality in the book of Acts. The Spirit empowers the church, distributing gifts and filling God's people for service and ministry. As a result, God's rule begins to work outward from Israel to the nations.

The Spirit forms a community as a witness of the salvation in the kingdom and a tool to extend that salvation to others. All people are invited to repent, be baptized, and receive the free gift of the Holy Spirit. In accordance with Jesus' promise (Acts 1:8), the church moves from Jerusalem (2:1–6:7) to Judea and Samaria (6:8–11:18) and eventually through the outlying parts of the Roman Empire to Rome itself (11:19–28:31).

God chooses Saul (whom we now know as Paul) to lead the missionary effort into the Roman world. His conversion (chapter 9) is a central event in the book of Acts. Controversy erupts as some Jews insist that non-Jewish converts to Jesus must obey the Law of Moses. God affirms His work among the Gentiles by giving Peter a vision (chapter 10). The church in Antioch becomes the first community of both Jewish and Gentile believers (11:19-21). From there, the church's missionary efforts among the Gentiles become more formalized under Paul's leadership (chapter 13 through 19:20). He establishes new churches throughout the Roman Empire (Romans 15:17-22). Paul establishes leadership in these fledgling communities, passes along scriptural and apostolic teaching, and institutes baptism and the Lord's Supper.

The church's new life and worshipful obedience are for the sake of world (see 1 Peter 2 and compare Exodus 19:1-6). As Paul endeavors to cultivate a community that faithfully embodies the new life of the kingdom, he never loses sight of those outside the church (Romans 12:17; Philippians 1:27; 2:15; 4:5; Colossians 4:5-6; 1 Thessalonians 4:12; Titus 2:7-8). The communal life of the church is to powerfully attract those who are outside of it. The witness of the church is to spill over into the public life of the culture, demonstrating the comprehensiveness of the salvation of the age to come.

7

The Offense of the Cross

*The truth does not change according
to our ability to stomach it.*

FLANNERY O'CONNOR

The story of redemption is the very heart of the biblical testimony about the work of God. Let's summarize what we've covered so far.

God began His mission to rescue and redeem humanity from the effects of the fall by calling Abram and forming the nation of Israel (Genesis 12:3). The story of Israel foreshadows what will be reality in Christ.

God sent Jesus Christ to accomplish this redemption. The Creator became the Redeemer. Through His death and resurrection, Jesus defeated the powers of Satan, sin, and death, making possible the reconciliation of all things to God. Jesus announced that God's redemptive work is present in the kingdom of God. As the second Adam, Jesus reverses the results of the first Adam's rebellion. The church stands as testimony that the powers and principalities that govern this world have been defeated.

God is currently working out the redemption of the world through the work of the Holy Spirit and the community He formed—the church. Those who are in this community are reconciled to the triune

God and to other people (inside and outside the church). The church does not exist for itself, but rather is sent by God back into the world to participate in God's mission to redeem all things. The church is therefore a witness to God's reign in the world and a sign or foretaste of the fullness and consummation of the kingdom.

As we move forward, I want to emphasize two points above all others. The first is that we must continually pay attention to the whole story line of scripture: creation, fall, redemption, and restoration. If we ignore the account of creation, we will either minimize our responsibility to care for the world or we'll elevate the environment in ways that confuse the creation with the Creator. If we ignore the fall, we will be too optimistic about the world's chances for self-improvement and too prone to baptize every seemingly good idea as kingdom work. If we ignore redemption, we will lose sight of the centrality of sin, Christ, the cross, repentance, and faith. And as we'll see later, if we neglect restoration, we will think of salvation simply as fire insurance for the next life.

The other major point of this book is that this story line subverts all the other narratives that govern our lives. In the story of redemption we see a God who comes near, a God who rescues us and the world from the sullied state we have created with our sin. Through Jesus, God is *with us* in ways we could never have imagined without the scriptures. God doesn't give up on us or on this world; He is at work to rescue, redeem, and restore. All of this is completely foreign to those who live only by our current narratives, but the form and shape that redemption took is the most bewildering thing of all.

The cross stands as the ultimate demonstration of God's subversive nature; there is no greater contradiction between the story of God and the stories of this world than this.

> For the message of the cross is foolishness to those who are perishing, but to us who are being saved it is the power of God... Since in the wisdom of God the world through its

wisdom did not know him, God was pleased through the foolishness of what was preached to save those who believe. Jews demand miraculous signs and Greeks look for wisdom, but we preach Christ crucified: a stumbling block to Jews and foolishness to Gentiles, but to those whom God has called, both Jews and Greeks, Christ the power of God and the wisdom of God. For the foolishness of God is wiser than man's wisdom, and the weakness of God is stronger than man's strength (1 Corinthians 1:18,21-25).

A Scandal

For Paul, the message of the cross is an offense, a scandal, something that looks foolish to the world. Paul recognized that the cross ran counter to every expectation (in every culture and every religion) of how God would make Himself known. This is completely surprising and unexpected. No one could have made this up.

The scandal of the cross continues to this day. Some ignore it, some ridicule it, and some try to reduce its shame. Long familiarity with it has lessened its absurdity and has led us into turning the cross into an item of beauty. Our problem is that we are too used to the Christian story; it is difficult for us to grasp the absurdity—indeed, the sheer madness—of the crucifixion. Peter Kreeft makes this point well:

> The incarnation was the biggest shock in history. Even his own people, whom he had prepared for two thousand years for this event, could not digest it... Even his own disciples could not understand him. It was the unthinkable...that the eternal God should have a beginning in time; that the maker of Mary's womb should be made in Mary's womb; that the first one became second, the independent one became dependent as a little baby, dependent for his very earthly existence... Even the devil did not expect this folly. That God should step right into Satan's trap, Satan's

world, Satan's game, the jaws of death on the cross; that he should give Satan the opportunity to cherish forever, in dark, satanic glee, the terrible words from God to God, "My God, My God, why hast Thou forsaken Me?"... That God should take alienation away from man by inserting alienation into the very heart of God; that he should conquer evil by allowing its supreme, unthinkable triumph, deicide, the introduction of death into the life of God... that he should destroy the power of evil by allowing it to destroy him—this is "the foolishness of God [that] is wiser than men, and the weakness of God [that] is stronger than men" (1 Corinthians 1:25).[1]

Those whose lives are shaped by the whole biblical story look at the cross and see God's glory, power, and victory. Others look at it and see a religious symbol of past and present oppression, outdated superstition, or cosmetic jewelry fashion. People of all kinds want to determine for themselves how they will personally come to God. Some say they can know God through philosophical speculation or religious experience. The cross demands we accept God on His terms.

For the Jews, the Messiah was to overthrow Israel's enemies in power. Many of Jesus' contemporaries asked Him to perform miracles or signs to prove He was the Messiah. Certainly His ministry was filled with such works, but Jesus saw the people's demands for the miraculous for what they really were: not sincere requests, but rather opportunities to test Him. Many of the Jews of Jesus' day incorrectly believed that if God were to visit this world, He would come in power and glory, crushing Rome. But the cross spoke of weakness, not power; defeat, not victory; humiliation, not conquest.

Nobody conceived of a crucified Messiah; only failed messiahs ended up on crosses. This was how Rome executed deluded fanatics who thought they were God's chosen heroes. The experience was as humiliating and ignoble as it was physically painful. Even Jewish law announced, "Anyone who is hung on a tree is under God's curse"

(Deuteronomy 21:23). The cross was the ultimate icon of Roman oppression. Asking a fellow Jew to boast about a cross was like asking a modern Jewish man or woman to boast about a gas chamber.

We make similar demands of God today. We insist that God should dazzle us into His kingdom. We look for bribes, formulas, or iron-clad promises for a healthy and wealthy life. We insist we will worship God if He'll heal us, provide for us, or give us what we want. But God makes no such deals.

An Embarrassment

The subject of crucifixion was an embarrassment even to the Romans themselves. It was a method of torture that combined pain with indignity, torture with humiliation. The victim was stripped naked, flogged within an inch of his life, and made to parade through the streets carrying the crossbeam to which his deformed and already mutilated body would be nailed when he reached the place of execution. Then he was held up to public view while enduring a long, drawn-out agony. This torture was reserved for only the lowest classes and was so embarrassing that polite Romans avoided speaking of it. If they couldn't avoid the topic, they would use euphemisms such as *unlucky tree.* According to Cicero, "The very word *cross* should be far removed not only from the person of a Roman citizen, but from his thoughts, his eyes, and hears." Josephus refers to this as "the most wretched of deaths."

The Greeks of Jesus' days demanded wisdom, so the idea of a crucified Messiah was absurd. If the powerful gods of Greece and Rome died, as some did, they braved a heroic death—full of mystique and majesty. They would never be humiliated like this. Greeks sought to know God by argument and rational principles—even the untrained thought this way. They wanted a god who made sense.

But Paul argues that vain human philosophy and religion has not known Him. The Jews, Romans, and Greeks all started their quest for God from the wrong place. Religious experience, signs, and philosophical speculation are all unable to reveal the salvation God provided through Jesus on the cross. Must God meet our demands, or must we meet His?

Yes, our demands for wisdom or signs continue. Like the Greeks, we want God to make sense, or like the Jews, we want validation through miracles and experience. But this demand itself shows that in our hearts, we are opposed to God's work in the world and calling on Him to fulfill our own expectations and demands. The notion that God would manifest Himself in human flesh and claim to save the world in such a barbaric way sounds like nonsense. How could someone be wise and powerful and still end up on a cross?

An Offense

The cross of Jesus is a monument to the depth and breadth of human sin and to the depth and breadth of God's holiness and love. Sin, death, and evil had infected the world so deeply that only the death and resurrection of God's Son could heal it. This is a central piece of the good news about Jesus: He has reconciled us to God and bridged the separation and alienation from Him that we were born into. But this good news subverts our attempts to save ourselves through our own understanding or religiousness. That is why it is so offensive.

It is historically offensive. The idea that a crucified God would save humankind has always been absurd to many. It is culturally offensive, as we have seen. The cross was never mentioned in polite first-century Roman society, and yet Paul emphasized its message, and Christians continue to glory in their mangled Messiah. It is philosophically offensive. Even today some complain that the cross is not an illustration of God's love but rather a form of cosmic child abuse. It is an offense to modern ears because it speaks of one death, one way to be right with God, not through our own striving or performing, but through Christ's death and resurrection. It is morally and religiously offensive because it confirms that because of the fall, we are incapable of saving ourselves and must be rescued instead. No one can brag about his or her fitness to be right with God based solely on their own merit.

This is the story handed down to us: Jesus suffered every imaginable horrific thing that could be done to anybody. He was questioned, betrayed, deserted, denied, spit on, struck in the face, slapped, mocked, stripped naked, insulted, beaten, lied about, falsely accused, convicted, condemned, crucified, humiliated, scorned, pierced, bruised, rejected, hated, stared at, left naked in public to die, and killed. Against all appearances to the contrary, Paul insists that this *is* the power (for the Jews) and the wisdom (for the Greeks) of God (1 Corinthians 1:24). This scandal was the greatest news one could hear, an embarrassment that unveiled the majesty of God and foolishness that was the greatest wisdom ever.

This is because, as the next verse says, the foolishness of God is wiser than man's wisdom. God's wisdom looked like folly, but it was not. His power looked like weakness, but it was not. The world around us thrives on selfishness, but God functions with sacrifice. He proved Himself mighty by taking on weakness. In His weakest state, when the world did its worst, He was victorious. He conquered suffering by suffering; He conquered death by dying and brought us life by rising from the dead.

Cross-Shaped Reality

To begin His plan to redeem the world He made, God called a man (Abram) and formed a nation (Israel) that produced the Messiah—the one who alone could bless all the nations of the world. That Messiah was Jesus, who came and lived among us in ways that we never expected. His death was a shock to His followers, even though He had repeatedly warned them about it. His resurrection was just as unexpected—and instructive. It not only validated that He is the Messiah but also set the pattern for the ministry that His disciples were to carry on through the power of His Spirit.

We live in a cross-shaped world. The things we naturally associate with strength (fame, riches, status, power…) turn out to be signs of weakness, and the things we naturally think of as indicators of weakness (humility, servitude, restraint, and mercy) may actually be signs of strength. God's values stand the values of this world on their head. What looks like defeat turns out to be victory, and what looks like foolishness is often true wisdom. In a cross-shaped world, blessing can come disguised as a Down syndrome child, the loss of a job, or a diagnosis that won't go away. All things are possible in a world where God saves by (seemingly) losing and gives life by dying. Things are not what they seem in such a world. When my wife and I found out Seth had Down syndrome, a couple with a four-year-old Down syndrome child told us with tears in their eyes that they were happy for us. *Happy* for us? But this is the kind of world the cross opens up—a world in which God can and often does turn things upside down.

Because of the cross and resurrection of Jesus, everything is different, and we are invited to live in contradiction to the world. If you want to live, you must die. Greatness means serving. The first will be last, and the last first. Saving your life means giving it away. It's almost as if to see the values of Jesus and His kingdom, simply take every natural human value or priority and flip it on its head. This great inversion subverts all the stories of our world—our fairy-tale classics, our Hollywood blockbusters, and our sports extravaganzas.

The cross defines the way we are to live together: without ego, self-promotion, or competition and comparison. We are all equally sinners and all equally in need of grace and rescue. None of us can justify ourselves before God, so we have no room for boasting, arrogance, or superiority. In the cross-shaped reality, we are insufficient and need help outside ourselves. Paul reminds his converts of what they were before God rescued them. He argues that God chose unimpressive people to negate the world's misplaced arrogance. This subverts our wrongheaded views of wisdom, power, reputation, and value. Nothing could be more subversive of power than the proclamation of a crucified man as the Lord of the universe.

The cross wars against the pride of our race, reminding us that at our core, we have no room to brag before God. This forces us to be humble and exposes us as posers and pretenders. Our wisdom is nonsense, our power is limited, and our goodness is insufficient. We must depend on God to save us. By choosing the lowly, God has forever ruled out every imaginable human system of gaining favor. We can either trust Him or...well, there is no other option.

The God Who Moves First

The cross and empty tomb shout out the shocking possibility of redemption to our hurting and sinful world. The God of the scriptures moves first, reaching out and pursuing. He does not stay away, creating the laws of nature and sitting back to watch what will happen. In the persons of the Father, Son, and Holy Spirit, the one God of the Bible directly intervenes in the affairs of humankind, offering hope and rescue. Redemptive history is a demonstration that God is determined to renew and reclaim what He has made in and through Jesus.

But this doesn't sit well with us. Adam and Eve's sin has crippled us beyond any human cure, but we would rather live autonomously and independently than humble ourselves and cry out for help. The cross shows that our best intentions, our most heartfelt actions, and our smartest ideas are not nearly enough to confront the problems of this world. Redemption comes only as we humble ourselves and acquiesce to our need.

Martin Luther famously contrasted this theology of the cross with what he called a theology of glory. Updating his language a bit, according to a theology of glory, God's job is to glorify us—give us wealth, success, or the fulfillment of our dreams. Jesus came (primarily) to heal us and to remove any obstacles to health and prosperity. God wants us to reach our potential, to be winners, to be all we can be.

The cross destroys the theology of glory. Jesus was simple and humble and submitted Himself in obedience to suffering. He didn't appear among us as popular, cool, or glorious. When God walked among us, He was different from what we expected. So do we go with the real Jesus or the one we really wanted? Do we let Jesus divinely reveal what God is like, or do we seek to know Him purely through religious experience or human speculation?

Christ's finished work is both individual and cosmic. It includes personal forgiveness and pardon for our sin as well as the final restoration of our bodies and the whole world. Christ restores our relationship with God and renews all of creation. But none of this is available for those who remain disconnected from Jesus. Sin's acidic curse remains on everything that continues to be separated from Christ.

The Victory of Love

Jesus' response to everything that happened to Him was to love, forgive, invite, care, and reconcile. Jesus chose to respond not with evil, but with good. Would He spit back? Would He curse His mockers, fight His torturers, and accuse His accusers? In every passage we see Him responding with love. He never becomes the evil that others did to Him. Instead, He responds with love and mercy every single time.

Jesus has overcome the world. The world works in a new way. If we think the cross *only* gets us out of hell and into heaven, we have missed the depth and breadth of its significance. Through the cross, God changed the way the world functions. Now that Jesus has defeated evil by living a perfect life, never once giving in to the temptation to return evil for evil, everything is different. He has overcome evil, and He gives me a share in that victory. When I desire to hurt those who have hurt me, I demonstrate that I am living according to the way the world *previously* worked. The cross and empty tomb invite me to live in this new world and to overcome evil with good.

Every day, we choose how we are going to respond to the world around us. Will we overcome evil with good? Or will we choose to get even? When people cut us off in traffic, will we react by returning the favor? When people say something hurtful, will we respond in kind? Our responses reveal the way we think the universe works. If it operates under the old order of things, we must repay evil for evil, or we lose.

The world and the demonic powers that rule it hit Jesus with everything they had. And at the end of that "good" Friday, they appeared to have defeated Him. They had seemingly triumphed over this pretender king of the Jews. But by Easter morning we learn the true score—Jesus alive and appearing to His followers! The apparent defeat was actually a reality-altering victory. Though it looked like foolishness, it was wisdom. Though it looked like humiliation, it was glory and love.

When we are mocked, persecuted, or treated badly and seem to be losing our battles with our families, friends, or coworkers, the cross assures us of the truth: We are winning! Jesus' crucifixion and resurrection changed the way everything works. Love and goodness triumph over evil, death, and sin. Our circumstances and the way people interpret them and talk about them (and talk about us!) are somewhat irrelevant. We can respond knowing that, in the end, Jesus triumphs and brings love, goodness, truth, and beauty.

8

The Beginning of the End
and the End of the Beginning

The creation waits in eager expectation
for the sons of God to be revealed.

Romans 8:19

Jesus' work on the cross and His resurrection from the dead accomplished a lot more than only securing Christians' tickets to heaven when they die. The events of that first Easter weekend have cosmic dimensions.

God determined to redeem (rather than destroy) what He has made, to reverse the curses of sin, death, and evil, and to renew and restore creation. God is on a mission to reclaim His corrupted world, redirecting it back to Himself and ultimately making everything new (Revelation 21:5). This redemption is both spiritual *and* physical, individual *and* corporate, and it leads to the transformation of this world into the one to come (Revelation 11:15).

The biblical teaching on the depth and breadth of redemption (what I am calling *restoration*) is quite different from what most of us have heard or been taught. We usually think of human history ending with our escape to an otherworldly existence in heaven, which is somewhere "up there." We're not sure what we'll do forever, but it probably has something to do with clouds, harps, streets of gold, and a very, very, very, very long church service. Of course, being with Jesus is better than anything we can imagine here, but the standard picture of heaven doesn't quite fire the imagination. And it leads to very thin understandings of hope, death, and heaven.

We were created to enjoy fellowship with God in the fullness of earthly life. In the creation narrative, we clearly belong with the created order and can fulfill our telos only as part of it, not separate from it.

When Satan tempted Adam and Eve to rebel against God, he tried to derail God's plan, and he succeeded in one sense—sin and its effects now touch all of creation. God set out to deal with sin and its consequences by destroying the enemy of His good creation, not by destroying creation itself. Redemption from sin must extend as far as the consequences of sin. As John proclaims, "The reason the Son of Man appeared was to destroy the devil's work" (1 John 3:8).

Salvation and restoration are comprehensive. In Christ, all the dimensions of human life and creation will be made new. For far too long, our view of salvation has been focused solely on our individual souls going to heaven after we die. Yet the enticing pictures we see in the scriptures reveal a creation that is renewed and restored to all of its goodness.

New Heavens, New Earth

At the end of the book of Revelation, we see the final picture of God's restoration: a new heaven and new earth cleansed entirely of sin and evil (Revelation 21:1; see also 2 Peter 3:13).[1] The old heaven and earth (infected by sin, death, and corruption) give way to a new order in which heaven comes to earth and God dwells forever with His people. The New Jerusalem comes down from heaven to earth. The kingdom comes, and God's will is done on earth as it is in heaven. All wills that are contrary to His are no more.

Revelation gives us a vision of a creation completely restored to its original goodness, rightness, and fitness for God's purposes. Sin and all its effects are gone; all four dimensions of *shalom* are reestablished. God lives intimately with His people, once again as close to us as He was in the garden. Relationships between people are restored. The whole of human life is purified. The goal of redemptive history is a renewed creation: healed, redeemed, and restored.

This vision differs substantially from what we have usually been taught. In the book of Revelation, Christians are not suddenly transported out of this world to live a spiritual existence in heaven forever. This is not taught in the New Testament. In this renewed world, the redeemed of God will live in resurrected bodies within a renewed creation, free from sin and its effects. Many scriptures hint at this:

- "Behold, I will create new heavens and a new earth. The former things will not be remembered, nor will they come to mind" (Isaiah 65:17).

- "He must remain in heaven until the time comes for God to restore everything, as he promised long ago through his holy prophets" (Acts 3:21).

- "For God was pleased to have all his fullness dwell in him, and through him to reconcile to himself all things, whether things on earth or things in heaven, by making peace through his blood, shed on the cross" (Colossians 1:19-20).

- "I tell you the truth, at the renewal of all things, when the Son of Man sits on his glorious throne, you who have followed me will also sit on twelve thrones, judging the twelve tribes of Israel" (Matthew 19:28).

- "The creation waits in eager expectation for the sons of God to be revealed. For the creation was subjected to frustration, not by its own choice, but by the will of the one who subjected it, in hope that the creation itself will be liberated from its bondage to decay and brought into the glorious freedom of the children of God" (Romans 8:19-21).

Nothing in creation escaped the effects of sin after Eden, and nothing in creation will remain unchanged by God's redemption after Christ's victory on the cross. Michael Wittmer agrees:

> Just as sin began with individuals and rippled out to contaminate the entire world, so grace begins with individuals and ripples out to redeem the rest of creation. We humans are the bull's-eye of God's grace, the target of redemption. But though salvation begins with us, the God who redeems us does not want us to keep our redemption to ourselves.[2]

So Revelation 21 pictures something that the rest of the Bible had already promised and hinted at. The Greek word translated *new* indicates that the new earth will be new, not simply as opposed to old, but that it will be new in quality and superior in every way—it implies continuity with our present earth and heaven (Paul uses the same word when referring to a new creation in 2 Corinthians 5:17).

The Resurrection of Our Bodies

For Paul, the resurrection not only validated Jesus' claims and teaching but also foreshadowed the renewed world. First Corinthians 15 is Paul's most extended treatment of Jesus' resurrection and its implications for us.

> Christ has indeed been raised from the dead, the firstfruits of those who have fallen asleep. For since death came through a man, the resurrection of the dead comes also through a man. For as in Adam all die, so in Christ all will be made alive. But each in his own turn: Christ, the first fruits; then, when he comes, those who belong to him. Then the end will come, when he hands over the kingdom to God the Father after he has destroyed all dominion, authority and power. For he must reign until he has put all his enemies under his feet. The last enemy to be destroyed is death. For he "has put everything under his feet." Now when it says that

> "everything" has been put under him, it is clear that this
> does not include God himself, who put everything under
> Christ. When he has done this, then the Son himself will
> be made subject to him who put everything under him, so
> that God may be all in all (1 Corinthians 15:20-28).

The Old Testament scriptures that Paul knew were like a story in search of an ending, and Jesus' resurrection was the ending. This was where it was going all along.[3] Jesus' resurrection launched the new creation, which now serves as the prototype for what God intends for our bodies and all of creation.

For Paul, Jesus' resurrection is not merely a spectacular event that confirms His special status before God. Rather, it is the beginning of a much greater harvest—the resurrection of all those who are in Christ. Jesus' resurrection is directly connected to our own (1 Thessalonians 4:13-18).

The Jews never expected just one man to be raised from the dead in the middle of human history. Their understanding of the end of the age included a resurrection for all, but this foreshadowing was a complete surprise. The Judaism of Paul's day did not include the expectation that the Messiah would die and rise from the dead. Instead, the Jews expected that a general resurrection of the dead would accompany God's judgment at the end of the world.

This presented an entirely new reality for the early Christians. They took the resurrection of Jesus as a sign that the end of the age had already started. If Christ was raised, then the resurrection of others must logically follow. Paul's metaphor of *firstfruits* serves to express the idea that the great harvest of the general resurrection will come in due course.

In 1 Corinthians 15:21-22, Paul takes a different tack to make the same point that Jesus' resurrection is not an isolated event. He compares the effects of Adam's sin with the effects of Jesus' resurrection. In the same way that Adam's sin brought death to all humanity, Jesus' resurrection broke the power of death and sin that had hovered over humanity since Adam. Adam stands at the gate of the old age, Jesus at the gate of the new. Adam's first sin inaugurated the present old age and brought sin, death, and condemnation. Now in Jesus, a new age of righteousness, life, and redemption has come (Romans 5:12-21). Jesus is alive, and the kingdom has come; therefore, the age to come has arrived. It is not an isolated occurrence, but the new creation is dawning in an overwhelming manner as a decisive transition from the old to the new world (2 Corinthians 5:17).

Paul is careful to see the church's present life in the interval between Christ's resurrection and His second coming. He argues that our resurrection must wait until Jesus returns again. Death is an enemy that will be defeated as Jesus destroys all opposition to God and returns everything to God's rule (1 Corinthians 15:24).

The resurrection is the work of God the Creator, and it will involve transformation and not merely resuscitation (1 Corinthians 15:36-38). God will complete the project He began at the beginning, and in the process, He will reverse and undo the effects of human rebellion, especially death itself, the great enemy that drags down God's beautiful creation into decay and dissolution. Our current bodies are naturally subject to corruption, dishonor, weakness, and death. Like Adam, they come from dust and eventually return to dust. But our new bodies will be like Jesus' glorified body—full of glory and power, never to die again. They will be immortal and incorruptible.

What We'll Do Forever

So this is the picture we get of the restoration, renewal, and redemption of all things in Christ. But not everyone will spend eternity with God on the new earth, and creation itself is not somehow divine. Instead, redeemed humanity will dwell with God on a new earth and in new bodies, doing very human things, forever. Notice some points of continuity and discontinuity with this present order of things. For one thing, there will be no sorrow, grief, or death in the new world.

- "On this mountain the LORD Almighty will prepare a feast of rich food for all peoples, a banquet of aged wine—the best of meats and the finest of wines. On this mountain he will destroy the shroud that enfolds all peoples, the sheet that covers all nations; he will swallow up death forever. The Sovereign LORD will wipe away the tears from all faces; he will remove the disgrace of his people from all the earth" (Isaiah 25:6-8).

- "I will rejoice over Jerusalem and take delight in my people; the sound of weeping and of crying will be heard in it no more" (Isaiah 65:19).

- "He will wipe every tear from their eyes. There will be no more death or mourning or crying or pain, for the old order of things has passed away" (Revelation 21:4).

Moreover, the scriptures say we will see Jesus face-to-face, whereas we now see dimly and know partially (1 Corinthians 13:8-12). There will be no more sickness, disease, or decay. The curses and powers that have governed this age will be destroyed. But there will also be continuity with this world.

Arise, shine, for your light has come, and the glory of the LORD rises upon you. See, darkness covers the earth and thick darkness is over the peoples, but the LORD rises upon you and his glory appears over you. Nations will come to your light, and kings to the brightness of your dawn.

Lift up your eyes and look about you: All assemble and come to you; your sons come from afar, and your daughters are carried on the arm. Then you will look and be radiant, your heart will throb and swell with joy; the wealth on the seas will be brought to you, to you the riches of the nations will come. Herds of camels will cover your land, young camels of Midian and Ephah. And all from Sheba will come, bearing gold and incense and proclaiming the praise of the

LORD. All Kedar's flocks will be gathered to you, the rams of Nebaioth will serve you; they will be accepted as offerings on my altar, and I will adorn my glorious temple.

Who are these that fly along like clouds, like doves to their nests? Surely the islands look to me; in the lead are the ships of Tarshish, bringing your sons from afar, with their silver and gold, to the honor of the LORD your God, the Holy One of Israel, for He has endowed you with splendor.

Foreigners will rebuild your walls, and their kings will serve you. Though in anger I struck you, in favor I will show you compassion. Your gates will always stand open, they will never be shut, day or night, so that men may bring you the wealth of the nations—their kings led in triumphal procession (Isaiah 60:1-11).

Behold, I will create new heavens and a new earth. The former things will not be remembered, nor will they come to mind. But be glad and rejoice forever in what I will create, for I will create Jerusalem to be a delight and its people a joy. I will rejoice over Jerusalem and take delight in my people; the sound of weeping and of crying will be heard in it no more.

Never again will there be in it an infant who lives but a few days, or an old man who does not live out his years; he who dies at a hundred will be thought a mere youth; he who fails to reach a hundred will be considered accursed. They will build houses and dwell in them; they will plant vineyards and eat their fruit. No longer will they build houses and others live in them, or plant and others eat. For as the days of a tree, so will be the days of my people; my chosen ones will long enjoy the works of their hands. They will not toil in vain or bear children doomed to misfortune; for they will be a people blessed by the LORD, they and their descendants with them. Before they call I will answer; while they are still speaking I will hear. The wolf and the lamb will feed together, and the lion will eat straw like the ox, but dust will be the serpent's food. They will neither harm nor destroy on all my holy mountain (Isaiah 65:17-25).

There is so much to notice here. The prophet says Jerusalem is to be a delight, pointing back to the garden of Eden (*Eden* means "delight"). The cultural mandate remains in effect (working, planting, building, and dwelling), but the curses will be reversed. Instead of work being painful, we will "long enjoy the works of [our] hands." In our resurrected bodies, we'll eat and drink, cultivate and work, and enjoy human life as it was intended to be. We'll make things and enjoy them. This sounds a lot like what God intended for humankind in the garden of Eden. It is not a vision of some other faraway and fuzzy realm that involves harps and clouds. Instead, the earth is restored, renewed, and reconciled. God Himself will bring heaven to earth (Revelation 21:1-4) and dwell with His people forever.

Isaiah 60 describes the new earth as a place of commerce, wealth, and the continued cultivation of human culture. God won't transform us into semiangelic beings who spend eternity pursuing monkish pursuits. Instead, we read of gold, houses, vineyards, work, and flocks. Our souls *as well as our bodies* are saved in God's new world. The earth and our cultural contributions to it carry forward from this world into the next.

We often talk about heaven as if it's not quite as real as the present universe. But according to the scriptures, the new heavens and earth aren't less real, they are more real (Hebrews 11:10). This is why C.S. Lewis called this world the shadowlands; everything here is but a shadow of what God intended because it is all tainted and twisted by death, corruption, sin, and decay. Life is less vibrant and real here in this world because death has touched everything. But take all that away, and we'll be more alive, more real, and more in touch with what we were supposed to be.

Biblical hope is universal in this sense. When scripture describes the end of human history, it includes all creation—lions and lambs, mountains and vineyards, nations and peoples. This all-encompassing vision of restoration is what we see throughout the Old Testament prophets. They dreamed of a new age in which people convert weapons of war into tools for harvest and children play safely with lions and snakes. Human cultural development and work will continue. The cultural achievements of history will be purified and will reappear on the new earth (Revelation 21:24-26). Humanity will continue to work and develop the creation but without the burden of sin.

The New Testament describes three major events that will usher in the restoration of creation and the arrival of God's kingdom in its fullness:

- Jesus returns,
- the dead are raised bodily (some to life in the new creation and others to final wrath), and
- the world comes before Christ to be judged.

These end-times events have often stirred endless (and often fruitless) controversy among Christians. As some have said, we should not be focused on the labor pains, but on the coming of the baby.

Life After Life After Death

*[Resurrection] wasn't a way of talking about life
after death. It was a way of talking about a new
bodily life* after *whatever state of existence one
might enter immediately upon death. It was,
in other words, life* after *life after death.*

N.T. Wright

I have attended many funerals, both as a pastor and as one of the
bereaved. I am writing this two days after my stepfather died—
nearly two years to the day after the death of my own dad. My limited
experience indicates that most Christians today lack any real sense of
where we are headed, other than going to heaven when we die. And
because of this, we really don't know how to grieve or offer hope to
others. We are a "card, casserole, and cliché" culture. Certainly, nothing
is wrong with those things. But is this the best we can do? A Hall-
mark card, some food after the memorial, and a nice "She's in a better
place"? I have heard some of the most well-intentioned but trite and
meaningless things said at funerals. Here are some statements I have
actually overheard:

- "God needed someone to make chili" (at a cook's funeral).
- "God needed someone to build mansions in heaven" (at
  the funeral of a contractor).

- "He's now fishing with Jesus" (my dad was an avid fisher-man).

You get the point. These aren't mean-spirited things, but surely we have more to offer.

The worst offender among clichés like these is this: "It must be God's plan." I heard this one from some very well-meaning church folks at my dad's bedside while he was withering away from cancer. I remained silent but thought to myself while looking at my father, *This is most certainly not God's plan.*

God's plan was for us to live with Him in Eden. His plan was for *shalom* to characterize our entire world: no sickness or death, sin or shame, fear or guilt. *This* was God's plan. Cancer certainly wasn't.

The idea of restoration subverts not only our cultural stories but also many of our Christian stories. For most of us, heaven is the fuzzy, ethereal destination where we do a lot of floating and harp playing. But the biblical picture is much richer.

Any system that portrays heaven as a fuzzy somewhere else is simply not in accord with the biblical description. We will spend forever on the renewed earth living in harmony with God—building, making, creating, working, celebrating, feasting, interacting with others—and with people who are living and working and pursuing what they enjoy. This is real life with death taken out.

Death, Paul writes, is the last enemy to be defeated. Death is an *enemy,* not an interruption or a mild setback we are to suffer through. The Bible also describes death this way:

- biologically—the common end to this life
- metaphorically—life apart from God
- theologically—a foreign power that invaded the world through Adam's rebellion.[1]

Death is part of God's judgment of His creation's sin (Genesis 2:17; 5:5; Romans 5:12; 6:23; 8). It is not natural to this world, nor was it part of God's original design for humanity. It is an enemy! It is to be grieved, lamented, and fought against. But Christians are to grieve differently than do those who have no hope.

Life After Life

The scriptures are unanimous in their testimony that our life extends beyond our physical death. We are physical-spiritual hybrids, so when our bodies die, our souls continue on, waiting for their reunion with our renewed physical bodies.

One of the central biblical themes of life after life is judgment— giving an account to God for what we have done during our lives on earth. Obviously, this is not a popular concept these days, but it echoes throughout the scriptures and most importantly in Jesus' teachings:

> But I tell you that men will have to give account on the day of judgment for every careless word they have spoken (Matthew 12:36).

> Not everyone who says to me, "Lord, Lord," will enter the kingdom of heaven, but only he who does the will of my Father who is in heaven. Many will say to me on that day, "Lord, Lord, did we not prophesy in your name, and in your name drive out demons and perform many miracles?" Then I will tell them plainly, "I never knew you. Away from me, you evildoers!" (Matthew 7:21-23).

> When the Son of Man comes in his glory, and all the angels with him, he will sit on his throne in heavenly glory. All the nations will be gathered before him, and he will separate the people one from another as a shepherd separates the sheep from the goats. He will put the sheep on his right and the goats on his left.
>
> Then the King will say to those on his right, "Come, you who are blessed by my Father; take your inheritance,

the kingdom prepared for you since the creation of the world. For I was hungry and you gave me something to eat, I was thirsty and you gave me something to drink, I was a stranger and you invited me in, I needed clothes and you clothed me, I was sick and you looked after me, I was in prison and you came to visit me."

Then the righteous will answer him, "Lord, when did we see you hungry and feed you, or thirsty and give you something to drink? When did we see you a stranger and invite you in, or needing clothes and clothe you? When did we see you sick or in prison and go to visit you?"

The King will reply, "I tell you the truth, whatever you did for one of the least of these brothers of mine, you did for me."

Then he will say to those on his left, "Depart from me, you who are cursed, into the eternal fire prepared for the devil and his angels. For I was hungry and you gave me nothing to eat, I was thirsty and you gave me nothing to drink, I was a stranger and you did not invite me in, I needed clothes and you did not clothe me, I was sick and in prison and you did not look after me."

They also will answer, "Lord, when did we see you hungry or thirsty or a stranger or needing clothes or sick or in prison, and did not help you?"

He will reply, "I tell you the truth, whatever you did not do for one of the least of these, you did not do for me."

Then they will go away to eternal punishment, but the righteous to eternal life (Matthew 25:31-46).

If we take seriously Jesus' words about prayer, love, and humility, we must also take seriously His words about judgment and hell. Jesus talks about hell more than do all other New Testament writers combined. Whatever else we may know about hell, we can be confident it is a real place where people go. We can debate the details, but the reality of judgment looms large over the eschatological framework of the New Testament. What we do in this life matters. One judgment separates those in Christ from those who are not in Christ, and another judgment evaluates Christians' work for Jesus while on earth. "For we must all appear before the judgment seat of Christ, that each one may receive what is due him for the things done while in the body, whether good or bad" (2 Corinthians 5:10).

Life After Death (and Life After That)

The Christian story announces that our deaths aren't the end of our lives. Contrary to those who suggest we simply return to the dust, the Bible announces that we die and then face judgment: "Just as man is destined to die once, and after that to face judgment, so Christ was sacrificed once to take away the sins of many people; and he will appear a second time, not to bear sin, but to bring salvation to those who are waiting for him" (Hebrews 9:27-28).

After we die, we go to be with Christ ("life after death"), leaving our bodies behind. We don't get much information about this in-between state (we may call it *heaven*), but we should not think it is the end of all things. After an interim period, we will receive resurrected bodies, fit for God's new world (life after life after death).[2]

God will not abandon this world; He will redeem it. When He restores and renews it, He will raise His people (those in Christ) to live in it in physical resurrection bodies. He is present with us now, but we see Him only partially and dimly. One day this veil will be lifted, heaven and earth will be rejoined, Jesus will be fully revealed and present with us, and every knee will bow and every tongue will praise him. The universe will be renewed, the dead will be raised, and all that God intended for His world will come to pass. Resurrection isn't a fancy name for life after death. Michael Wittmer comments, "Heaven is more suitable for spiritual beings and angels and human souls—bodies are meant to live here, on this planet."[3]

What We Do in the Meantime

Despite what you may think, the point of faith in Jesus isn't going to heaven when you die. Both the Old Testament and the New Testament demonstrate that God intends restore creation to His original purposes for it. Our story does not end with our souls leaving our bodies and fleeing our world; it ends with heaven coming to earth with God dwelling among His people (Revelation 21:3). This gives us hope, perspective, and purpose and summons us to live in the present as people of the future.

We have received God's blessing and redemption so that we can participate with God and dispense those things to others. God not only saves us from our sin but also rescues us to actually do something. We are to bear witness about God's redemption. Our embodied communities proclaim and demonstrate the good news of God's kingdom. Our work concerns not only the salvation of individual lives but also the renewal of our culture. God allows us to carry forward His work of restoration into the structures and systems of the world. The cultural mandate continues to apply, so we are still called to develop the world around us for God's glory. God designed churches to be instruments of renewal and reconciliation in the world—not only of individual lives but also of cultural forms and structures, helping to make straight all that is crooked in the world.

God commissioned His people to serve as His agents of renewal, with our own resurrection serving as the pattern for the resurrection of all creation. Jesus gave us the Great Commission to bring every part of our lives and every part of our world under His lordship. When we do, we bring the renewing power of God's reign and rule on earth as it is in heaven. God's ultimate purpose for Christians is not to bring them out of this world and into heaven but to use them to bring heaven (where God's will is done) into this world.

Here is an important point of clarification: We could never usher in the consummation of God's kingdom. We are not working under the illusion that we are capable of solving the world's problems. Only Jesus can heal, redeem, judge, and restore the world. Our obedience matters, as do our effort, worship, and faithfulness to Jesus. Our good works will not go unnoticed or unrewarded. But we cannot achieve any utopia or bring in the kingdom now because sin is still in the world. Only Christ can usher in His kingdom, which He will do when He returns again.

This means we must walk between two opposite and equal errors. On the one hand, we must avoid triumphalist thinking that somehow we can bring the fulfillment of God's kingdom to earth. The best of our efforts and intentions will never remove the stain of sin and death that is attached to everything. But on the other hand, even though we will not bring about the final consummation of the kingdom, we should not think that our efforts are in vain. The promise that God will bring about His new world is precisely the reason why our work on the earth matters. Notice how Paul connects our work on earth with our future life in God's new world:

> I declare to you, brothers, that flesh and blood cannot inherit the kingdom of God, nor does the perishable inherit the imperishable. Listen, I tell you a mystery: We will not all sleep, but we will all be changed—in a flash, in the twinkling of an eye, at the last trumpet. For the trumpet will sound, the dead will be raised imperishable, and we will be changed. For the perishable must clothe itself with the imperishable, and the mortal with immortality. When the perishable has been clothed with the imperishable, and the mortal with immortality, then the saying that is written will come true: "Death has been swallowed up in victory."
>
> Where, O death, is your victory?
> Where, O death, is your sting?
>
> The sting of death is sin, and the power of sin is the law. But thanks be to God! He gives us the victory through our Lord Jesus Christ.

> Therefore, my dear brothers, stand firm. Let nothing move you. Always give yourselves fully to the work of the Lord, because you know that your labor in the Lord is not in vain (1 Corinthians 15:50-58).

We cannot heal every hurt, correct every injustice, or remove every evil, but we are still called to be active participants in bringing God's reign and rule to earth as it is in heaven. We can be ambassadors of *shalom* in our families, workplaces, schools—wherever God has put us, so that we become a sign and foretaste of the kingdom that has come and is coming, that is "here but not yet."

As we have said, Christ's finished work includes both individual and cosmic dimensions. These range from personal forgiveness, cleansing from sin, and the final restoration of our bodies, to the renewal of the whole world. Christ has restored our relationship with God and is renewing all of creation. None of this is available for those who remain separated from Jesus. Sin and death continue to ruin everything that remains disconnected from Christ.

> The way most Christians think about redemption is more influenced by Greek philosophy than by the Bible. We think of ultimate redemption as being redemption from the body, not of the body; redemption from the world, not of the world; redemption from the material, not of the material.[4]

So the work of the church includes both evangelism and cultural renewal. We summon people to faith in Christ, and we work to redirect creation and culture toward God's original intention for it. When God's people invest themselves into the world through education, business, or politics, or when they advocate for and develop created goods like marriage or medicine, they become instruments of God's redemption.

Michael Wittmer's words provide a fitting summary of the message of this chapter:

Nowhere does Scripture hold out heaven as our ultimate goal. Instead, it informs us that heaven is merely the first leg of a journey that is round trip. The Christian hope is not that someday we get to join our Christian friends and family in the presence of God, but that God will bring our loved ones with Him when He returns to live with us on planet earth. In short, we earthlings were made to live here—on this planet. This is where we belong. We're already home.[5]

PART 3

Your Place in the Story

A New Way of
Seeing the World

*I believe in Christianity as I believe that
the sun has risen; not only because I see it,
but because by it I see everything else.*

C.S. Lewis

How do we find our place in the great, grand biblical story? Our response begins with *faith*. Faith is not a blind leap, not believing in the irrational, and not merely acknowledging something to be true. Faith is much bigger, deeper, and greater than that. Faith primarily is a way of seeing the world. Faith allows us to enter into the story, right in the middle of the twenty-first century. "Faith is being sure of what we hope for and certain of what we do not see," writes the author of Hebrews (11:1). Paul acknowledges, "We live by faith, not by sight" (2 Corinthian 5:7). Both passages contrast faith with sight. *Sight* here refers to trusting in what we see with our eyes. Biblical faith sees the world beyond what we can perceive with our five senses.

This isn't the way most of us understand and use the term. In the modern lexicon, *faith* is synonymous with *opinion, hope, wish,* or *belief*. It is certainly does not count as anything remotely resembling knowledge. But our popular understanding of faith is not biblical, nor is it practical. Very few of us scrutinize our beliefs every moment of every day. When I cross a busy street, I simply trust that my eyes are conveying an accurate picture of the world and step into a crosswalk. I don't spend a lot time speculating on whether the road is an illusion or whether the drivers in the other cars are real. I just simply assume what I see to be accurate.

This sort of presumption, governed by commonsense pragmatism, is what the Bible refers to as faith. Biblical synonyms for *faith* include *trust, certainty,* and *assurance.* It adds no hint of a blind leap of faith into something irrational or absurd.

So faith is not solely the property of the religious believer. It is what enables all of us to live healthy, productive lives. Atheists, agnostics, scientists, Buddhists, and Christians all have faith (trust, confidence) in something. It may be technology, themselves, money, karma, or whatever, but none of us lives by mathematical or logical certainty all the time. This is most certainly true of our relational lives. Who among us could boil down friendships, children, or lovers to simple algebra? No, there is a knowing, a trusting, a kind of faith that takes place when we are in relationship with another human being. These stand beyond our control and our dominion.

When we say the Bible presents an alternative reality—an alternative story, in Ivan Illich's terms—we must receive this by faith. This doesn't mean we will never have questions or doubts but that we fundamentally trust that the scriptures narrate a story that accurately describes the way the world really is. Biblical faith is never opposed to doubt—it is opposed to sight. In this sense, *sight* means trusting only in that which our senses convey to us, that which we can touch, see, hear, taste, or smell. This is the predominant way of seeing and knowing in the twenty-first-century Western world.

> We need to say that the heart of our life lies in our faith, and getting this right is tremendously important—not so we can get points for being right but so we can interact successfully with reality. That is how faith saves us. Our

faith in Jesus Christ enables us to integrate our lives with his life in a way that makes the resources of God's kingdom pour into our lives. When you have a correct faith that you have fuel in your [car's gas] tank, your reward is not that you believe the right thing. Your reward is that your trip to town works, and you don't wind up stranded somewhere... People who believe in the virgin birth do not get points for believing in the virgin birth. They live in a different world—a world where virgin births occur is a different world from one in which they don't. A world where Jesus Christ rises from the dead, a world where we have a reliable word of God in the scriptures...this is different from a world where these things aren't true. And when we believe we live in the true world, we gain the riches and realities that God has provided. When we don't believe we live in that world, we are simply restricted to what we can work out on our own.[1]

The scientific method has become the primary filter for knowledge in Western culture. Something counts as knowledge only if we can know it scientifically. If we can't, we classify it as a value, opinion, or preference. And as the modern story goes, none of us can claim one value, opinion, or preference as privileged over another. We are all entitled to our opinions because they don't qualify as knowledge in the proper sense.

What I am suggesting flatly contradicts this. We have knowledge of all sorts of things that are not quantifiable, repeatable, or measurable. The methods and content of the sciences certainly add to our ability to relate accurately to the world, but humanity has much more at its disposal that this.

I know I love my wife, that I ate breakfast this morning, and that my children exist. What we can know about the world is much broader than the modern story would have us believe. Faith is one of the ways of knowing what the modern story leaves out.[2]

So to say, as I am suggesting, that the Bible presents us with a narrative that we embrace by faith, I am not saying we should receive the biblical story unquestioningly or blindly. Nor am I advocating a return to modern fundamentalism ("The Bible says it, and that settles it"). Instead, we must step into this story, act on it, and experience it before we can fully know it. This story is self-validating and self-reinforcing. Jesus argues as much in John 8:31: "If you hold to my teaching, you are really my disciples. Then you will know the truth, and the truth will set you free." We must step into it and personally participate in it in order to see its truth.

The biblical story does not reinforce the modern stories surrounding us today. In fact, it is in direct conflict with the narratives guiding twenty-first-century life. It is not a creed to be recited, a liturgy to be performed, or a set of doctrine to be memorized. This is an entirely different way of seeing the world and our participation in it. It is not for the fainthearted or those who want the Bible in nice pithy chunks. The story demands a response, be it one of faith, trust, and obedience, or one of disquiet and neglect.

Belief in the scriptures is always tied to how one lives. The writers of the New Testament could not have conceived of believing one thing and living another. They lived what they believed and believed what they lived. To believe something was, by definition, to live accordingly.

Jesus' invitation to us is not primarily to memorize a set of doctrines, recite a specific creed, or perform a rote liturgy. Those have their place. But Jesus calls us to *live* under God's gracious rule and reign in dynamic and interactive relationship with Him. His forgiveness of us is not the end of our journey with Him. It's only the beginning.

As a central aspect of this life, this journey with Christ, we pass on to others what we ourselves have received. We forgive as Christ forgives us. We love as Christ loves us. We comfort with the comfort we receive from God. We are ambassadors of the message of reconciliation, just as we have received and accepted it ourselves.

This understanding of our calling in Christ is essential to living out the gospel. In the New Testament, those who follow Jesus are called saints, ambassadors, ministers, and priests. Empowered by God's Spirit and equipped with spiritual gifts, we are invited to reflect Jesus' love, grace, and truth to the world.

If I believe in God but reject a God-informed, God-directed life, what is the nature of my belief? Practically speaking, do I believe in a God who I believe is unworthy of belief?

Seeing the World the Way Jesus Did

The call to faith is an invitation to see the world the way Jesus saw it. This does not mean checking off a certain set of doctrines or propositions. Rather, it means living and interacting with the world as if reality were a certain way. The biblical story invites us to believe that it is the true story of the world and that every other story is a smaller reflection of the grand narrative of the Bible. To enter God's kingdom we must believe in Him, but to grow in His kingdom, we must look at the world the way Jesus did. As Dallas Willard suggests, "As his apprentices, we pass through a course of training, from having faith *in* Christ to having the faith *of* Christ (Galatians 2:16-20)."[3]

This is much more than learning new information. Learning to see something this way is akin to learning to see in agriculture, business, art, or sports. I have played and coached football. When I watch a game with my wife, she and I see it differently. She sees a bunch of men running around banging away at each other, and I see audibles, adjustments, schemes, and strategies. The reverse is true with basketball. For the life of me, I can't figure out what counts as offense in hoops, but my wife watches a game and comments on the various plays the teams run. I have to take her word for it because I don't see a thing.

We constantly find differences between what experts see and what the uninitiated see. I look up and simply see wispy puffs of white, but a meteorologist sees stratus, cumulous, or cirrus clouds. I go to the zoo and see cats, monkeys, gorillas, and reptiles, but a zoologist sees each animal in particular and can tell you the difference between an alligator and a crocodile. I see only a field, but a farmer sees the crop, notes its variety, and assesses its health.

When we step fully into the story, we receive eyes to see. When we accept and participate in that mercy, our eyes are opened to categories of creation, sin, world, reconciliation, kingdom of God—the categories by which we see reality as it really is. This is anything but natural or automatic. Rather, learning to see reality this way requires induction and immersion into a culture.

Think of it as being adopted into a new family. Assuming a new identity, understanding the dynamics of the new family, trusting the goodness of new parents…these require time and participation. We must be molded and trained in certain ways in order to see what is really happening around us.

Faith is acting as if these things were true. It is not only a matter of thinking or speaking (although it includes those things). Faith is primarily a matter of acting. That is why James claims that faith without works is dead. It's ineffective.

Looking at Things We Can't See

Three broad themes are central to Jesus' view of reality. First, Jesus clearly believed in the reality and importance of the unseen, spiritual world (Matthew 6:9; Luke 10:18; John 4:21-24). To Jesus, the spirit world was far more real than the world of the senses, and God was the most pervasive being in all of reality. This is hard for us to accept because we are bombarded with precisely the reverse idea. The only things we can know are things we can physically see, and they are somehow more important than invisible things. Jesus always used the invisible world to interpret the visible world, not the other way around. We see this in Jesus' view of demonic activity and spiritual warfare. Jesus believed that two kingdoms—the kingdom of God and the kingdom of Satan—are at war with each other (Matthew 12:22-29). He cast out demons and pointed to His exorcisms as proof that His kingdom was at work (Luke 11:19-20).

Jesus shows us that the most important thing is to align ourselves with what God is doing in our world. The unseen world is the fundamental reality. The modern church sometimes communicates that God is one of the things we use to make our lives successful, so we assign Him a place in our a toolbox right alongside college degrees, jobs, personalities, and the like. Jesus saw the world the opposite way: We exist to discover how to get on board with God's program, not the other way around. Your life will never be a success if you spend all your time and energy trying to figure out how Christianity can help you. Your life will be a success, however, if you (like Christ) are preoccupied with how you can invest your talents and treasures in the kingdom of God. (Of course, you will also need to determine what *success* means in God's kingdom—which leads to our next point.)

Kingdom Reality

Second, Jesus' ministry and teaching centered around the coming of the kingdom of God (Mark 1:14-15). In the Old Testament, God selected one man, Abraham, out of the whole earth. God promised three things to Abraham: a new land, a great nation of descendants, and blessing that he would pass on to all the peoples of the world. The rest of the Old Testament develops this idea. Jesus announced that the kingdom of God was now available. The kingdom of God is an invisible community of people who live under God's rule. In the Old Testament, that kingdom was not directly available to everyone. Citizens of that kingdom had to go through priests, a sacrificial system, and protocol. When Jesus says that the kingdom is available now, He is saying that you can enter the kingdom of God right where you stand, and you can experience life with God whatever your station in life is. The good news includes much more than forgiveness of sins alone—it is the good news of the presence and availability of life in the kingdom, now and forever, through reliance on Jesus Christ.

The Big Problem

Third, Jesus' taught about the wickedness of the human heart (Mark 7:14-15). People didn't understand this teaching because it was so radical. They thought that food could make them unclean, that their public behavior made them acceptable to God. Jesus revealed that the problems in society begin in our own hearts. The craziness around the Jews had little to do with Assyria, Babylon, Rome, Caesar, Herod, Pontius Pilate…instead, they were rooted in the wickedness of the human heart. This is the most important thing that will keep us from enjoying life in the kingdom—the readiness to do evil that lies under our hearts. Religious behavior does not touch the wickedness of my heart—only Jesus can do that.[4]

Transformed by the Words, Spirit, and Community of God

Life in the kingdom of God involves an interplay between a person, the Bible, the Holy Spirit, and the church (community) of God.

In combination with the Spirit of God and the community of God, the narrative of the Bible can enter into our lives as we enter into it. This is why God repeatedly urges His people to immerse themselves in scripture:

- "Do not conform any longer to the pattern of this world, but be transformed by the renewing of your mind. Then you will be able to test and approve what God's will is—his good, pleasing and perfect will" (Romans 12:2).

- "You diligently study the Scriptures because you think that by them you possess eternal life. These are the Scriptures that testify about me, yet you refuse to come to me to have life" (John 5:39-40).

- "Let the word of Christ dwell in you richly" (Colossians 3:16).

- "Your attitude should be the same as that of Christ Jesus" (Philippians 2:5).

- "I am the vine; you are the branches. If a man remains in me and I in him, he will bear much fruit; apart from me you can do nothing… If you remain in me and my words remain in you, ask whatever you wish, and it will be given you" (John 15:5,7).

- "His delight is on the law of the LORD, and on his law he meditates day and night. He is like a tree planted by streams of water, which yields it fruit in its season, and whose leaf does not wither" (Psalm 1:2-3).

- "The weapons we fight with are not the weapons of the world. On the contrary, they have divine power to demolish strongholds. We demolish arguments and every pretension that sets itself up against the knowledge of God, and we take captive every thought to make it obedience to Christ" (2 Corinthians 10:4-5).

- "Set your minds on things above, not on earthly things" (Colossians 3:2).

Our world trusts so exclusively in what we can see with our five senses, we must continually allow the words, Spirit, and community of God to reorient us to the reality of Christ and His kingdom. As I have said, this is not a matter of learning new information (though that may happen). Rather, when we sit under the power of the Bible, the Holy Spirit does the deep work of transformation. The Spirit gives us a clearer apprehension of the truth (John 15:26; 16:8-15; 1 John 2:27) beyond what those who do not have Christ can understand (Matthew 13:14-15; 1 Corinthians 1:18).

The Spirit also applies the scriptures to the depths of the human heart. Paul informs us that the word of God is the sword of the Spirit (Ephesians 6:17). Therefore, as Hebrews 4:12 tells us, the word of God is living, active, and sharp. Thus, it penetrates and judges thoughts and attitudes of the heart. The Spirit applies the truth of the scriptures to us deep in our hearts (Romans 8:15-17). Dallas Willard frames the power of God's word:

The literal truth is that Christ through his word removes the old routines in the heart and mind—the old routines of thought, feeling, action, imagination, conceptualization, belief, inference—and in their place he puts something else: his thoughts, his attitudes, his beliefs, his ways of seeing and interpreting things, his words. He washes out our minds, and in the place of confusion and falsehood—or hatred, suspicion and fear, to speak of emotions—he brings clarity, truth, love, confidence and hopefulness.[5]

This work of the Spirit, however, does not take the place of immersing ourselves in the scriptures. Nor does it mean that "you do not need anyone to teach you" (1 John 2:27). The same Spirit has gifted some for a teaching ministry in the church (Romans 12:7; 1 Corinthians 12:29; Ephesians 4:11). Teachers can help us understand the scriptures, but they are not required mediators, nor can they place the word deeply in our hearts. When the words of the scriptures get inside us—whether directly or indirectly—they deal with our true souls and form a life that is congruent with the world God has created, the salvation He has enacted, and the community He has gathered. God uses these words to form the mind of Christ in us.

As Eugene Petersen explains, *spirit*-ual writing requires spiritual reading, a reading that honors the words as holy, that allows the words to form an intricate web of relationships between God and the human, between the visible and invisible. A different kind of writing (personal and relational rather than informational and impersonal) requires a different kind of reading (slow and attentive, rather than aloof and efficient). [6]

All of this happens in community. The Bible was never meant to be read, interpreted, and practiced alone. As many have said, the *you*'s are plural. That is, most of the commands of the New Testament are written to churches and not to individuals. Therefore, one of the primary roles of the church is the enculturation of people into the new humanity, the people of God. Others may define us by outward appearance or position, but the community of God is to be the place where we are treated without regard to externals—the place without the prejudice, discrimination, or favoritism of the world. Through worship, our imaginations are refreshed and reoriented around the goodness, majesty, and power of God. Through Bible reading and study, we are grounded in the truth about God, our world, and ourselves. Through communion, baptism, and liturgy, we tell and retell different parts of the story. We must immerse ourselves in the Trinitarian reality of God so that His true story can subvert the images, values, priorities, and stories of the world.

Stepping into God's Story

*Man the image bearer is somehow involved in the
shaping of the history that God ultimately controls.*

DAVID G. HEGEMAN

*Human history is no longer a human
affair. It is Someone Else's project.*

DALLAS WILLARD

The Bible narrates God's mission to restore creation. Israel's mission
flows from this. God chose a people to embody His creational
purposes for humanity and to be a light to the nations. The Old Testament narrates the history of Israel's response to their divine calling.
Jesus comes on the scene and takes upon Himself Israel's mission. He
embodies God's purpose for humanity and accomplishes victory over
sin, opening the way to a new world. When His earthly ministry is
over, He leaves His church with the mandate to continue in that same
mission. In our own time, standing as we do between Pentecost and
the return of Jesus, our central task as God's people is to witness to
the rule of Jesus Christ over all of life.[1]

The nation that came from the line of Abraham, Isaac, and Jacob
(or Israel) was to embody God's original intention for humanity and
creation (Exodus 19:3-6). As Israel was obedient to God, it was faithful

to its calling to be a light to the world. But Israel didn't faithfully live up to its calling. Jesus came and fulfilled God's purposes for Israel, and then He gathered a community of disciples and gave them the work of continuing what He had begun (John 20:21).

This is where N.T. Wright's five-act drama structure provides great help:

> Suppose there exists a Shakespeare play whose fifth act had been lost. The first four acts provide, let us suppose, such a wealth of characterization, such a crescendo of excitement within the plot, that it is generally agreed that the play ought to be staged. Nevertheless, it is felt inappropriate actually to write a fifth act once and for all: it would freeze the play into one form, and commit Shakespeare as it were to being prospectively responsible for work not in fact his own. Better, it might be felt, to give the key parts to highly trained, sensitive and experienced Shakespearian actors, who would immerse themselves in the first four acts, and in the language and culture of Shakespeare and his time, and who would then be told to work out a fifth act for themselves.
>
> Consider the result. The first four acts, existing as they did, would be the undoubted "authority" for the task in hand. That is, anyone could properly object to the new improvisation on the grounds that this or that character was now behaving inconsistently, or that this or that sub-plot or theme, adumbrated earlier, had not reached its proper resolution. This "authority" of the first four acts would not consist in an implicit command that the actors should repeat the earlier pans of the play over and over again. It would consist in the fact of an as yet unfinished drama, which contained its own impetus, its own forward movement, which demanded to be concluded in the proper manner but which required of the actors a responsible entering in

to the story as it stood, in order first to understand how the threads could appropriately be drawn together, and then to put that understanding into effect by speaking and acting with both innovation and consistency.[2]

Wright dramatically portrays our role in the story. We step onto the stage having learned the first four acts and are now living in the midst of the fifth. The New Testament gives us the beginning of the fifth act, and as we have seen, we know how it will end. Our job now is to continue the story that Jesus and the disciples began. Jesus said to His disciples, "As the Father has sent me, so I am sending you" (John 20:21). The kingdom mission that began with the calling of Abraham, continued with Israel, and culminated in Jesus is our mission today.

This is why we must pay attention to the whole Bible—the entire scriptural story. We must look back to the Old Testament to acquaint ourselves with Israel's God and His ways. To understand our own mission as the church today, we must immerse ourselves in Israel's calling and vocation, see how Jesus then fulfilled it, and note the way the early church began to understand itself in light of this work. To quote Wright again, "We read scripture in order to be refreshed in our memory and understanding of the story within which we ourselves are actors, to be reminded where it has come from and where it is going to, and hence what our own part within it ought to be."[3]

So Great Salvation

Many people believe that Jesus founded one of the great religions of the world. But despite popular opinion, a clear reading of the gospel accounts show that He intended no such thing. He did not come to begin what most folks call Christianity: a two-hour-a-weekend experience that religious people try to fit into their otherwise crazy lives. Jesus came announcing a *kingdom*—the subversion of every aspect of life and culture in order to bring it under God's good rule. When we live under God's administration—in His kingdom—our lives are brought into alignment with reality. To live in the kingdom of God is to have eternal life (John 17:3), and this life begins the very moment you begin to follow Jesus. Much harm has been done to the message of Jesus by presenting Christianity as a system of beliefs rather than as a way of life. Of course, it is both, but this overemphasis excludes discipleship (learning to live with Christ) from our understanding of salvation. If the gospel is only the message that Jesus forgives me and gives me a ticket into heaven, why should I worry about how I live now? Our traditional understanding of the biblical story doesn't answer this question very well. The term *Christian* occurs only three times in the New Testament, but the word *disciple* appears more than 270 times.[4] In fact, Jesus' standard invitation in the New Testament is "Follow me." The gospel writers include it 90 times.

When Christianity is our way of life, we restructure and reorient everything in our lives to be consistent with the way of Jesus. Knowledge, education, romance, marriage, sex, parenting, work, play, money, ambition, business, social services, caring for the earth, being the church in the world...all of these and a thousand more come under kingdom rule and authority. When we follow Jesus faithfully, we allow the story of the kingdom to subvert the old ways we process all of these, and we begin following the pattern of living that Jesus and His earliest disciples established.

Through the cross and empty tomb, Jesus secures God's victory over sin, death, and corruption. Jesus' work reverses the effects of the fall and grants the benefits of kingdom life to those who put faith in Him. He has made us active participants in God's work as we proclaim and embody the good news of the kingdom. To follow Jesus is to step into the big story of God. Creation, fall, redemption, and restoration can be our story too.

All human beings are created and fallen, but not all are redeemed and restored. In one sense, we step into God's story by abandoning our old lives and giving ourselves completely to God and His kingdom. But in another sense, all people step into God's story regardless of whether they know or acknowledge what is happening. Here's the difference: Those who intentionally follow Jesus step into the story at the point of redemption.

The Presence of the Future

Many first-century Jews divided human history into two distinct stages: this present age and the age to come. In their minds, the present age is dominated by sin, evil, oppression, and death, and it will come to an end when God's Messiah comes. His coming will usher in the age to come, in which God returns to Israel in power and glory, the Holy Spirit comes, the dead are raised to life, and Israel returns from exile.

But as we have seen, no one was expecting the crucifixion and resurrection of just one person—God's Messiah—right in the middle of human history. Yet Jesus provided unmistakable signs that the age to come had broken into the present age. The kingdom arrived in Jesus, but it is still waiting for its consummation upon His return. This is the starting point for Paul: The kingdom of God, the age to come, arrived in Jesus! Paul preached that the salvation promised by the Old Testament prophets has begun. The old age is passing away, and the new age is dawning (2 Corinthian 5:17-20). The fullness of time has arrived (Galatians 4:4), and today is the day of salvation (2 Corinthians 6:2).

Still, Paul was puzzled. If the new age has broken into the present through Jesus' life, death, resurrection, and ascension, why do sin, evil, and death still remain in the world? Paul (following Jesus' teaching in His parables) taught that we live in a tension. We live between the *already* (the new availability of the kingdom in Jesus) and the *not yet* (the day of consummation and restoration when Jesus returns). The kingdom has come and is coming. Jesus' death brought an end to the rules and powers of the old age, and His resurrection is the beginning of the new world.

Paul's view of the Holy Spirit is very important in this regard. He describes the Spirit as a deposit (down payment) on the coming kingdom (2 Corinthians 1:22; 5:5; Ephesians 1:14). He also pictures the Spirit as firstfruits, the beginning of the harvest and tangible evidence that the remainder will come in due time (Romans 8:22-25).

The Holy Spirit empowers Jesus' disciples to be, in very small measure, what Jesus Himself was—God's future arriving in the present and the means of God's kingdom filling the earth. The Holy Spirit comes as an appetizer (or foretaste) of the new world.

But the kingdom has not arrived in all its fullness, so we live in a world that is not yet fully cleansed from sin, evil, and demonic power (2 Corinthians 4:4). We are surrounded by sin and rebellion, so Paul calls this world "this present evil age" (Galatians 1:4). Yet we wait for the day when God will wipe those things away. Paul realized that we live in the in-between time—we are God's people, filled by His Spirit, right in the middle of the present age. In us the two ages overlap. Paul explains that God allows these two ages to coexist so that the church can accomplish its mission—the gathering of the nations to the God of Israel—before the full and final revelation of the kingdom.

In that sense, the church is "the presence of the future." We are God's on-display people, living according to the vision, values, and priorities of God's new world even though we still live and struggle within the present sinful age. We are a sign in the present of what is to come in the future (Ephesians 1:14). We are new creations (2 Corinthians 5:20), and our redemption makes us part—even now!—of the world to come. That is why Paul's commands to the churches are always based on the work God has already done in Jesus. Paul continually exhorts God's people to live up to what they already are (1 Corinthians 5:7; Ephesians 4:1). He declares first what God has done, and then he calls us to live in light of it. Our new birth changes our status in God's great story. The world of the Bible is our world, and its story of redemption is our story. This story is waiting for an ending—in part because we just play our part before the end can come. We must continue the biblical story of redemption.

The Cruciform Life

Our part in the story also takes on the patterns, priorities, and agenda of Jesus' work in the world. He doesn't join our stories; we join His. In repentance, we give up our right to govern our lives, and we submit to His will for us. This brings us under His good reign and rule, and our lives begin to show the goodness of living in God's world God's way. That is what it means to deny ourselves, take up our crosses, and follow Jesus. We are to give ourselves away for the sake of God's agenda in the world. I'm telling a story by the way I live—even if I'm not trying to and even if I don't know I'm doing it. We reenact God's story through our stories. We take upon ourselves Jesus' self-sacrificial calling to love and serve the world. We are to answer evil with goodness and love, just as Jesus did. We are to follow the way of humility and meekness, not the way of status and power. This is missing from most of our church communities. We don't recognize that our best response to Jesus is to look more and more like Him in the world. Our witness is communal and empowered by the Holy Spirit, but each of us who calls on Jesus is an active participant.

Our participation takes its shape from the cross of Christ. Jesus used His journey to Jerusalem as an aid in teaching this to His disciples. He suffered and was persecuted, and we can expect the same. He also graphically pictured His mission by washing the disciples' feet and redefining the Passover meal.

To follow Jesus is to follow Him in His mission. There is no way around it. According to the wisdom of God, the way to flourish is to give your life away; the way to fulfill yourself is to spend yourself; the way to be great is to humbly serve. To live according to God's story is to die with Christ and rise again (Romans 6:1-11). This is pictured in baptism at the beginning of our journey with Christ. We die (consistently and definitively) as the way of repentance and renunciation to our old self and the old age and powers that governed it. We rise again as the presence of the future, demonstrating the goodness of life with God and living under God's great narrative.

This present world will war against those who try to live according to the new order that Jesus inaugurated. Suffering and persecution are the inevitable result. We who follow Jesus come in His name, bearing His healing and redemptive touch. But the powers that presently rule this world have a vested interest in maintaining the current order of things.

The Real World

We need to be clear about what it means to follow Jesus if we are to fully enter into the journey. Being a Christian has little to do with memorizing creeds, debating abstract theological ideas, or singing songs. To follow Jesus is to present our real self in all its aspects to God, to depend on His Spirit, and to be used by Him for His work in the world. We seek first His kingdom, and in so doing, we serve as God's agents of renewal. Our own resurrection foreshadows the resurrection of all creation. God has commissioned us to bring every part of our lives and of our world under Christ's governance. When we do this, God's will is done on earth as it is in heaven.

Jesus' resurrection introduced a world in which a new type of justice is possible. Restorative justice is a primary aspect of the Christian calling to work for healing. Violence and personal vengeance are ruled out. At every level of life, every Christian is called to work for a world in which people experience reconciliation and restoration. As we do, we anticipate that day when God will indeed put all things back into accordance with His will.

Our Place in the Story

*The purpose of God with human history is nothing
less than to bring out of it—small and insignificant as
it seems from the biological and naturalistic point of
view—an eternal community of those who were once
thought to be just "ordinary human beings." Because of
God's purposes for it, this community will . . . pervade the
entire created realm and share in the government of it.*

DALLAS WILLARD

Every human community lives under some comprehensive story
that defines, governs, and unifies life in that community. Church
communities are no different in this regard. I have been suggesting
(along with many others) that the biblical story is the truest, most
significant and meaningful account of who God is and what He has
done throughout human history. We must constantly fight to make
sure this story shapes the way we see the world and not the other way
around (our world must not shape the way we see the story). One way
to do this is to build our church communities on this entire story and
not focus on small, devotional pieces of the Bible. Unless we do this,
we will likely be fitting the Bible into our story instead of fitting our
story into it. We have insisted that the dominant stories of modern
life share a common idolatry of self that insists that we human beings
are able to achieve our own salvation.

The Bible is important for the believing community, not as an oracle or magic formula, but as the document that bears witness to fundamental experience without which its members cannot understand themselves and their world. Everyone has such a document or collection of texts. They are often an unacknowledged anthology of readings, experiences, and events that have been stuck together with scissors and paste. The point is that everyone lives from some sort of "text" or "script." The Bible is the major text of Christians. It provides the architecture of our thoughts.[1]

In the past hundred years, the seeds of individualism and privatization have produced a crop of twenty-first-century Western Christians with an inordinate focus on the self as the main expression of the work of Jesus. I have a personal relationship with God; I engage in personal devotional time (consisting of me, a Bible, and Jesus); I engage in personal evangelism, personal prayer, and personal spiritual formation. I think the Bible's story is about what Christ has done for *me*, in *my* place, paying the price for *my* sins. *I* am forgiven, *I* have eternal life, and Christ now lives in *me*. *I* invited Jesus into *my* life and *my* journey so Jesus would walk with *me* and bless *my* life.

Of course, all of this is true, and we should never minimize the application of Christ's work to each individual who believes in Him. But as a result of this overemphasis, we have lost an understanding of and appreciation for the communal aspects of Christian life and faith that permeate the entire biblical story. Our expressions of worship, obedience, devotion, and witness are all primarily to be done in community. Communities are made up of individuals, of course, but the communal aspect of following Jesus is mostly foreign to us.

At almost every step along redemptive history, God forms a community of people and puts them on display. In the Old Testament, God forms Abraham's descendants into the nation of Israel. God could have responded to the catastrophes of the flood and Babel in various ways, but He created a community that would live under His rule and be a light to the nations.

Throughout the Old Testament, the people of Israel recounted a communal faith to their children. It was not a testimony of God's personal relationship with one particular individual but rather a story about God leading and responding to the community.

Many generations later, Jesus of Nazareth came as the fulfillment of Israel's story and mission. He gathered a community of disciples around Himself and gave them authority and power to work in His name, testifying to Israel the new availability of God's kingdom. After His death, burial, and resurrection, Jesus commissioned His followers to tell the nations what they had seen and heard. After His ascension, He poured out His Spirit to empower them and validate their witness.

To reiterate, in each movement of the redemptive story, God called a *community* to embody His salvation and proclaim it to the nations. Jesus said that the most powerful testimony of His work and grace would be the unity and love His church displayed.

Jesus established His church to be a foretaste of the restoration that awaits the rest of the world, to be a vanguard or beachhead of the kingdom of God among other rebellious kingdoms, to be a small piece of *shalom* amid conflict and division. God's intent has always been for His people to embody life under His rule so that others may be drawn in.

That is why I believe that what the world needs most from the church is for it to simply be *the church*—an increasingly distinctive community that embodies the good news of Jesus to each other and to our culture. That has been God's plan all along; to gather a collection of people who declare the works and wonders of the Savior, Jesus.

Because the triune God created human beings in His image, we are designed to be in relationships. We are generally at our best when we connect with and live our lives alongside of other people. As we have seen, the only thing that was not good in the creation account was that the man was alone. We were made for each other.

New Testament faith is never solely an individual concern. The New Testament rarely addresses itself to individuals. Individualism dominates our contemporary Western culture, but it is not the primary way God has spoken to His people. The vast majority of commands, exhortations, corrections, and directions in the letters of the New Testament are directed to communities of believers. Much harm has been done by filtering the Bible through a primarily individualistic lens.

An Embodied Communal Witness

In the New Testament, the word *church* never referred to a building or set of programs, but a community of people bound together by Jesus Christ. Our salvation was not intended to be simply a "me and Jesus" sort of thing. The gospel is announced most powerfully and its implications are worked out most effectively in a community of people. To speak rightly about the church, we must begin by talking about people and about relationships—with God and with one another. The best way to understand the church is to view it as a community.

We live in the biblical story together. We must understand how we fit in the main story line: We live between Christ's first coming (His birth, life, death, resurrection, and ascension) and His second coming (the judgment and the renewal of all things). We have referred to this as the *already* of Christ's first coming and the *not yet* of His second coming. This is the place the church occupies in God's story.

The church's current role in God's story is to be a witness. *Witness* means much more than simply evangelism or missionary work. When we grasp that God's plan for His administration is to restore all creation, we realize that our witness to His government is as wide as creation. *Witness* includes embodying God's renewing power in politics and citizenship, economics and business, education and scholarship, family and neighborhood, media and art, leisure and play.

We do this together. Jesus overcomes every division—ethnic, religious, socioeconomic, and the like—as He reconciles people to God and to each other. This community represents a new humanity that bridges the divisions between Jew and Gentile, male and female, slave and freeman (Galatians 3:28; Ephesians 2:14-18). The unity of God's people is to be the ultimate picture of the gospel to the world. Jesus prayed for all who would believe in Him: "I pray...that all of them may be one, Father, just as you are in me and I am in you. May they also be in us so that the world may believe that you have sent me" (John 17:20-21). Much of the New Testament's ethical teaching is summed up in the "one anothers" of life together. As God has loved, forgiven, and comforted us, we respond to His grace by loving, forgiving, and comforting others, sharing with them that which we ourselves have received. Spiritual maturity does not happen in isolation, but occurs in the furnace of our relationships to one another (see Ephesians 4:11-16). This communal and interdependent understanding of spiritual life and witness cuts against the prevailing view of spiritual life present in most churches today. Most of us in the church still try to grow in Christ using a do-it-yourself, paint-by-numbers approach that involves only ourselves and God. Despite the Bible's repeated insistence that our relationship to God can flourish only in the soil of our love for others, most of us still believe we can work it all out on our own. We must come to see the church, and our place in it, differently so that we may participate in the story in the ways the Author intended.

God is redeeming the world through the work of Jesus, the ministry of the Holy Spirit, and the fellowship of His church. The church is reconciled into relationship with both the triune God and with others. The church does not exist for itself; God sends the church back into the world to participate in His mission to redeem all things. The church is therefore not only a witness of God's influence in the world but also a sign or foretaste of the fullness and consummation of His kingdom on the renewed earth.

The church witnesses to and eagerly awaits Jesus' return, at which time Satan, sin, and death will be destroyed and God will dwell forever on earth with a renewed humanity. The reconciliation that Jesus accomplished is focused on human beings, but all creation will be redeemed as well (Matthew 19:28; Acts 3:21; Colossians 1:20).

The purpose of the church, then, is to present ourselves individually and corporately to God for the sake of advancing His kingdom into the world (Romans 12:1-2). We no longer exist for ourselves, and though we engage in study, prayer, worship, and service for our own benefit, we also recognize that those things serve a much greater purpose: They form us into people who can cooperate and participate with God in His work in the world.

> The gospel, you see, is not just a message for individuals, telling them how to avoid God's wrath. It is also a message about a kingdom, a society, a new community, a new covenant, a new family, a new nation, a new way of life, and therefore, a new culture. God calls us to build a city of God, a New Jerusalem. Remember the cultural mandate. Sin does not abrogate it. The gospel creates new people, who are committed to Christ in every area of their lives. People like these will change the world. They will fill and rule the earth for the glory of Jesus. They will plant churches and establish godly families and they will also establish hospitals, schools, arts, and sciences. That is what has happened, by God's grace. And that is what will continue to happen until Jesus comes.[2]

Understanding the gospel involves more than affirming a set of propositional truths. The gospel radically transforms our lives. It calls us to be empowered by the Holy Spirit—not as wandering loners, but as members of a community that is transformed and compelled by the gospel. Our task in living together as a gospel community is to accurately portray the heart and the glory of God.

> Although we may never fully succeed in restoring shalom to our selfish world, there is at least one place where we

should expect to find the flourishing, wholeness, and delight that comes from genuine community. Christ intends his church to be a herald of shalom. When this collection of diverse individuals chooses to sacrificially serve one another in the name of the Prince of Peace, we silently announce to a troubled world that the kingdom of shalom is present in our midst. In this way we proclaim the gospel of Jesus Christ, proving by our conduct that sin does not have the last word, but just as shalom once permeated the original creation, it has come to Christ's church and will come again to the world.[3]

When God set out to redeem His creation from sin and its effects, His goal was to completely restore what He created—to bring it back under His good authority, where it could live and thrive. Jesus Christ announced that goal (Luke 4:18-19) and then accomplished it (John 17:4; 19:30). The New Testament, as we have seen, declares that redemption is complete already even though we await its consummation. The Bible narrates God's progressive march toward this final restoration. It also reveals, piece by piece, what the final restoration will look like when it comes.

But the Bible gives us even more than a description of the future and a foundation of hope. It reveals the end of the story and invites us to participate in its unfolding. After Paul explains his carefully crafted theology of our resurrected bodies and Jesus' defeat of death, he brings his discussion back to the flesh-and-blood world of here and now: "Therefore, my dear brothers, stand firm. Let nothing move you. Always give yourselves fully to the work of the Lord, because you know that your labor in the Lord is not in vain" (1 Corinthians 15:58).

God will transform this present world into the world to come and renew and restore every part of creation (including our bodies). Therefore, our present stewardship of creation (including our bodies) is extremely important. Our future hope and present responsibility are intertwined.

To Paul, being heavenly minded includes being deeply engaged here and now. The resurrection and the restoration of all things reveal some degree of continuity between our current world and the world to come.

Earlier in 1 Corinthians 15, Paul repeatedly argues that if Jesus did not rise from the dead (as the beginning of the general resurrection to come), Christians' faith and work are meaningless. After spending most of the chapter arguing for the validity and importance of Jesus' resurrection, Paul affirms with equal vigor that our work for and with God in this world is not in vain. Because of the restoration and resurrection to come, everything we do now has worth and meaning.

The Kind of Story It Is

*It is enormously important that we see the role of scripture
not simply as being to provide true information about,
or even an accurate running commentary upon, the
work of God in salvation and new creation, but as
taking an active part within that ongoing purpose.*

N.T. WRIGHT

In a world that discredits any claim for one story to be *the* true story of the world, how can we claim that the biblical story trumps the others? Faith is not simply a blind leap into the irrational, so what basis does anyone have of even suggesting that one story is big enough to hold them all?

First, we must recognize that we all live within narratives that govern our lives. This is inescapable. We are inherently narrative creatures. Even the postmodern story, which discredits the existence of any overarching story, is itself an overarching story. We all live with deep questions about our origins (where do we come from?), identity (what are we?), and destiny (where are we headed?). Our view of the world shapes and is shaped by the grand story we see ourselves a part of.

This leads to the rather obvious judgment that some stories are truer than others. The story we may tell about Santa Claus differs from the stories we tell at family reunions. The stories my stepfather told about the Korean War are different from Hollywood's war stories. What follows from this is simply that we all look for marks of truthfulness in the stories we hear. When a movie begins with the phrase "based on a true story," we listen and watch differently than we would if the story were pure fiction. If a story begins with "Once upon a time" or ends with "and they lived happily ever after," we know what sort of story we are being told. If we say, "Two men walk into a bar…" most of us know a joke is coming. When we read the words "Long, long ago, in a galaxy far away…" we know to expect a Star Wars movie.

A work of fiction, for instance, operates differently from a work of history. A novel is different from a work of history, which is different from a lyric poem, and so on. Different genres make different kinds of truth claims. If I am reading a book of history and find out that some of it was simply made up, I won't trust it because of the kind of book it purported to be. But if I discover that C.S. Lewis invented the Chronicles of Narnia with no basis in reality, the novel isn't diminished, because its genre doesn't require historical precision. Different genres follow different rules.

To say the Bible is true is to say that what it intends to convey is true—and this (what is means) is shaped by (among other things) the genres it includes, the attitudes it takes to history, and the ways cultural contexts shaped the meanings of the words it uses. As we have seen, we have a bit of work to do to ensure we are understanding what it is saying to us before we judge its truthfulness. Thus, to say a particular passage is true is to say we can trust it as a guide to faith and life that provides not only specific claims about God's faithfulness and how we ought to live our lives in response to it but also a way of understanding the whole world.

In part, we trust the Bible because we find that it keeps making sense of the world in which we live. The Bible lays out a richly diverse vision of the world from beginning to end, and says, in effect, "This isn't some imaginary world, like Lewis' Narnia. This is the real world." Your life and the events around you thus will make sense only as they have their place within this great and grand story. And Christians find that, if they keep reading this book and living their lives in the context of the community that reads it, that promise keeps getting fulfilled in unexpected ways. We trust the Bible because we have come to trust the God about whom it tells us.

When we examine the Bible, what we find depends a great deal on what we bring with us during the examination. The Bible presents itself to us as an accurate picture of God, ourselves, and God's work in the world. It claims, in other words, that we should take it seriously because it reveals reality in ways we can't know apart from it.

> Many have undertaken to draw up an account of the things that have been fulfilled among us, just as they were handed down to us by those who from the first were eyewitnesses and servants of the word. Therefore, since I myself have carefully investigated everything from the beginning, it seemed good also to me to write an orderly account for you, most excellent Theophilus, so that you may know the certainty of the things you have been taught (Luke 1:1-4).

> Jesus did many other miraculous signs in the presence of his disciples, which are not recorded in this book. But these are written that you may believe that Jesus is the Christ, the Son of God, and that by believing you may have life in his name (John 20:30-31).

> We did not follow cleverly invented stories when we told you about the power and coming of our Lord Jesus Christ, but we were eyewitnesses of his majesty (2 Peter 1:16).

> For the appeal we make does not spring from error or impure motives, nor are we trying to trick you. On the contrary, we speak as men approved by God to be entrusted with the gospel. We are not trying to please men but God, who tests our hearts. You know we never used flattery, nor did

we put on a mask to cover up greed—God is our witness. We were not looking for praise from men, not from you or anyone else (1 Thessalonians 2:3-6).

That which was from the beginning, which we have heard, which we have seen with our eyes, which we have looked at and our hands have touched—this we proclaim concerning the Word of life. The life appeared; we have seen it and testify to it, and we proclaim to you the eternal life, which was with the Father and has appeared to us. We proclaim to you what we have seen and heard, so that you also may have fellowship with us. And our fellowship is with the Father and with his Son, Jesus Christ (1 John 1:1-3).

We see that the Bible claims to speak of things that really happened and life as it really is. It does not claim to be a fairy tale with a good moral lesson, or something that happened apart from real, flesh-and-blood human experience. It claims to be a faithful record of God's saving work in the world. We must begin at this point. This is not presented to us as one of several pictures of God and reality. It comes to us simply assuming that it is the one true story of the world.

The God Who Is

Before we look at the specifics of the narrative structure of the Bible, we need to put into place one last piece of background information. The Bible presupposes the presence of a personal, nonphysical being of great power and knowledge who is real and who created our world. If the statistics are correct, most of us share this belief.

What we believe about God determines (more than any other factor) how we will interpret the Bible. The Bible reveals a world of miracles, faith, wonders, signs, and supernatural power. Is that an accurate description of the world? Is the universe closed, operating according to its own fixed, immutable laws, or is it open to God's actions in human history?

How will we read the Bible? That depends on our response to the first four English words: "In the beginning God." If God exists, then virgin births and resurrections from the dead are possible. If He doesn't, then the Bible is just another great human myth, a legend of enduring inspiration.

The Beauty of Both/And

The Old Testament scriptures grew out of an ancient Near Eastern consciousness that is as foreign to our world as is Middle Earth. Likewise, the New Testament flourished under the Hellenistic and Roman influences that shaped the world outside of Israel, though the gospels retain much of the thinking, worldview, and hope we see in the Old Testament. For shorthand's sake, I'll refer to this way of seeing the world as the Hebrew or Jewish worldview. The Western world has inherited many of the Greek philosophical traditions, so I'll refer to our modern, common way of understanding as Greek or Hellenistic. Of course, these ways of seeing share many things in common. (If they didn't how could we even talk about them?) But the differences are significant enough to shape the way we approach the Bible.

Central to Jewish thought is the ability to hold both sides of a paradox simultaneously. A paradox is different from a contradiction. A paradox is a statement that seems contradictory but is nevertheless true. The key word in that definition of paradox is *seems*. A paradox is different from a contradiction in that a contradiction contains two statements that are opposed to each other. For example, "Mike is bald and has a full head of hair" is a contradiction because both statements cannot be true. In a paradox, half of the statement *seems* to be false but isn't. So "Mike is bald and has hair" is not a contradiction because he could have hair elsewhere. (I'll spare you the details.)

We find this sort of reasoning (called *halakic* reasoning) all throughout the Bible.[1] Jesus is fully human and yet fully divine. Not one or the other, but both. God is one, and yet the Father, Son, and Holy Spirit are all divine. God is both fully just and fully merciful. God chooses us and we choose God. Many matters central to Christian faith require us to hold in tension two seemingly contradictory truths about God and the way He works.

For those of us reared in the Hellenistic approach to reasoning, this takes some getting used to. For many, truth is supposed to be propositional, linear, and unambiguous. The answer is A or B, not both. And, most of the time, it is. But we get into trouble when we read the Bible without properly holding in tension the truths about God. Sometimes, all that we can say about both sides of an issue is that scripture teaches both, and leave it at that.

We could say much more about this, but for now, getting a little more comfortable with *halakic* reasoning will help us understand the Bible's view of itself. The scriptural writers often insist that they are inspired, that they are recording the very words of God.[2] Here are just a few examples.

> All Scripture is God-breathed and is useful for teaching, rebuking, correcting and training in righteousness, so that the man of God may be thoroughly equipped for every good work (2 Timothy 3:16).

> We did not follow cleverly invented stories when we told you about the power and coming of our Lord Jesus Christ, but we were eyewitnesses of his majesty. For he received honor and glory from God the Father when the voice came to him from the Majestic Glory, saying, "This is my Son, whom I love; with him I am well pleased." We ourselves heard this voice that came from heaven when we were with him on the sacred mountain.

> And we have the word of the prophets made more certain, and you will do well to pay attention to it, as to a light shining in a dark place, until the day dawns and the morning star rises in your hearts. Above all, you must understand that no prophecy of Scripture came about by the prophet's

own interpretation. For prophecy never had its origin in the will of man, but men spoke from God as they were carried along by the Holy Spirit (2 Peter 1:16-21).

We also thank God continually because, when you received the word of God, which you heard from us, you accepted it not as the word of men, but as it actually is, the word of God, which is at work in you who believe (1 Thessalonians 2:13).

This was not mere dictation, however. God didn't hand the Bible to humanity in finished golden tablets or override the authors' personalities by mechanically moving their hands. The Bible was written by people, about people, and for people. We see differences in theme, voice, grammar, and tone. We see that Paul's vocabulary was much different from Peter's and that Jeremiah's personality was much different from Samuel's. Much of the New Testament addresses churches dealing with flesh-and-blood issues, living in concrete first-century social contexts, and working out their discipleship to Jesus.

Of course, Jesus' incarnation shows how the human and divine intermingle. The scriptures teach that Jesus was fully human *and* fully divine. With some significant differences, we may roughly say the same thing about the Bible. God fully inspired the writing of the scriptures, but He used human beings to do it.

Written by People

From the very first pages of the Bible, God delegates some of His responsibility for running things. Not because He needs to, of course, but because He made us in His image, which includes participating in the taming of creation and taking it forward (the creation mandate).

Think carefully about what this means. God allows us the privilege of managing creation. Could He do it better? Of course! Adam was originally just a clod of dirt, and a few verses later, he's God's vice-regent on the earth. But the interesting thing is that this pattern of divine/human partnership winds its way throughout the scriptures.

Sex provides the best example of our participation in creation. When two people become one flesh, the union of their individual identities produces new life. We are minicreators in that regard.

In the third act of the Bible's story (redemption), God begins to redeem humanity by selecting a man (Abram, or Abraham) and forming his descendants into a great community. This community's job was to put God on display to the rest of the world (Exodus 19:4-6). They were to show what life was like under God's administration. In this way, God intended that they be a light to other nations.

God ruled His people through judges, prophets, priests, and kings. He could have done it better Himself—through angels or divine skywriting, maybe—yet over and over again, He gives people the responsibility and privilege of willingly joining with Him in His work in the world.

When God called the Israelites to settle in the land He had promised to give them, He initially fought other nations on their behalf. But to help them mature, He taught them to fight their battles as He empowered them.

Jesus walked the earth as a human being, drawing a few simple peasants and fishermen to follow Him and forming them into a movement that He empowered to change the course of human history. Now the Spirit of Jesus lives in people in every nation around the world, and He continues to work through them as His hands and feet.

This is what God does. He doesn't work around us; He works through us and with us. And so it makes perfect sense that as He recorded His revelation to and through His people, He included them in the process. This means that the Bible didn't fall out of the sky perfectly formed one day, nor did God simply dictate what He wanted said. Rather, He employed the divine-human partnership. God inspired the authors of scripture. He didn't force His thoughts on them but rather guided, led, enlightened, and provoked them so they could deliver the messages He had for His people. This process included the authors' individual personalities, experiences, perspectives, and the like. So, for example, reading Paul is different from reading Moses or David or Peter or James. They all differ in style, vocabulary, grammar, and the like. This is exactly what we should expect from a God who insists on communicating *with* people *through* people.

So to fully understand the biblical writers' messages, we must know the authors and their settings, situations, and cultural contexts. Biblical scholar Gordon Fee makes this point well:

> It is the doctrine of inspiration, that God inspired not only the people who spoke but also the words they spoke, that distinguishes the evangelical view of Scripture, and also forces us to wrestle with issues of hermeneutics [i.e., how we interpret the Bible]. Inspiration maintains that God indeed "spoke these words and said..." But it does not maintain that He dictated all these words. To the contrary, it recognizes, indeed argues, that these words are also the words of people in history... None of the words was spoken in a vacuum. Rather they were all addressed to, and conditioned by, the specific historical context in which they were spoken.
>
> To see Scripture as both human and divine creates its own set of tensions...God did not choose to give us a series of timeless, non-culture-bound theological propositions to be believed and imperatives to be obeyed. Rather He chose to speak His eternal word this way, in historically particular circumstances, and in every kind of literary genre.[3]

Written About People

The Bible is actually more than a story about people. It's a story about *God,* and it involves people. We aren't center stage at all. The Bible is primarily a written record of a God who determined to redeem His people. It isn't a story of our search for God, but rather of God's search for us.

But the scriptures do take an unflinching look at the objects of God's affection. In this way, the Bible is much more honest than are most of its followers. It records with unnerving detail the flaws, sins, and frailties of the people its talks about. Abraham's deceit. Moses' excuses. David's adultery. Solomon's immorality. Peter's denials. Only Jesus comes out looking any good.

The Bible is messy because it records God's relationship with messy people. It is a testimony to His goodness, greatness, and grace, which He chooses to display to us and through us. Much of what the Bible records it also condemns. Sexuality is once again the prime example. Though God clearly designed sexuality to be expressed in heterosexual, monogamous marriage, the scriptures record the polygamy, concubines, infidelity, and prostitution of many of the so-called heroes of the Bible.

The history of Israel unfolds the same way. The Old Testament is the progressive witness of Israel's glorious successes and stunning failures. Much of biblical literature was birthed out of Israel's disobedience. The prophets railed against injustice, greed, and idolatry. The wisdom literature, including Proverbs, Job, and Ecclesiastes, makes no sense apart from the suffering, conflict, and mistakes that God's people can learn from to become wise. As Israel practiced obedience in fits and starts, God responded in different ways. Sometimes He was like a master rebuking a servant. At other times He was like a groom romancing his bride. Occasionally He was like a parent punishing a child. God responded to His people's reactions to Him. He was constant, but they were not, and He related to them accordingly.

Frederick Buechner writes beautifully about the daunting challenge and the compelling attraction the Bible represents:

> [We could say that] it is a disorderly collection of sixty-odd books which are often tedious, barbaric, obscure, and teem with contradictions and inconsistencies. It is a swarming compost of a book, an Irish stew of poetry and propaganda, law and legalism, myth and murk, history and hysteria. Over the centuries it has become hopelessly associated with

tub-thumping evangelism and dreary piety, with super-
annuated superstition and blue-nosed moralizing, with
ecclesiastical authoritarianism and crippling literalism...

And yet—

And yet just because it is a book about both the sub-
lime and the unspeakable, it is a book also about life and
the way it really is. It is a book about people who at one
and the same time can be both believing and unbelieving,
innocent and guilty, crusaders and crooks, full of hope and
full of despair.

In other words, it is a book about us.[4]

Although the Bible is composed of many different literary styles
and a variety of themes, it presents one story—the story about God,
who created us, loves us, and seeks to redeem us.

Written for People

This may seem obvious, but the implications are significant. For one
thing, it means that God condescends to our level when He speaks.
When He spoke to Moses, He spoke Hebrew, the language of the nation
of Israel. The Greek of the New Testament writings isn't the polished
Greek of scholars and poets; it is the common Greek of the day. In the
Old Testament, God used the covenant practices of ancient Near Eastern nations to frame the Mosaic covenant. He used everyday images
to communicate deep truth—a pile of rocks marked the place where
God parted the sea, Passover lambs stood for deliverance from oppression and freedom to worship, manna (breadlike wafers that appeared
to Israel in the wilderness) reminded Israel of its dependence. The same
thing was true of Jesus—fishes, nets, pearls, swine, seeds, soils, har-
vests...all were images of the kingdom of God. He set His parables
and teachings firmly within the cultural setting of His day.

Paul's writings also bear the unmistakable imprints of cultural accommodation. God seems to be passionate about communicating in means,

pictures, images, and words that are readily accessible to us. Many of these are culturally dated and make little sense to modern ears. In fact, the progressive nature of God's story not only accommodates to our humanity but also causes a bit more work for us who are thousands of years removed from scripture's historical events and cultural contexts.

This means we should expect some mystery in the Bible. If God is who He says He is and we are who He says we are, then God and His ways are partly and necessarily beyond our comprehension. Doesn't God admit as much to Job? Job pleads for an answer to his suffering, and God's answer boils down to this: If you can't understand what I am doing in the physical universe, which you can see, you surely can't understand the working of the spiritual universe, which you can't see. We should not be surprised that some parts of the scriptures are hard to understand.

We can draw another conclusion from the fact that the Bible was written for people: It was written within and to specific communities of faith. Several parts of the Old Testament were written for Israel in exile. Recognizing this context is essential to understanding these writings. Many of the letters in the New Testament were written to first-century churches in Asia Minor. Digging into these churches' nature, their makeup and cultural setting, is essential if we are to make sense of the epistles. The Bible was their Bible before it was our Bible. This means that the simplistic "what does this verse mean to me" method for understanding the Bible can lead us into serious error. God is so great that He can speak through anything or anyone, but much of the Bible was written to specific people in specific places for specific reasons, and if we ignore this, we do so at our peril.

To be true to the Bible's view of itself, then, we must uphold both sides of this tension. Why can I trust the Bible? Because God superintended the process by which the Bible was put together (more on that later). Why was that process so messy? Because God included human beings in the process as preachers and teachers, storytellers and historians, prophets and poets, compilers and copyists.

Many of us seem to emphasize one element and ignore the other. For some, the Bible has no human element—it comes to us as a static or frozen piece of literature, so understanding it doesn't require a knowledge of history, culture, language, canonicity, or transmission. God said it, I believe it, and that settles it. Others of us miss the divine element, so the Bible is simply another great piece of literature to be studied, dissected, and categorized the same way as every other great book. Ignoring the human element leads us to blindly and uncritically accept the words in our English Bibles as if God wrote them directly to us. Ignoring the divine nature of the Bible leads many to an overly critical skepticism that leaves no room for faith or the power of God to provide us with a trustworthy record of what He is like and what He has done. Dallas Willard beautifully expresses the balance between the human contribution and the divine contribution to the Bible:

> On its human side, I assume that it was produced and preserved by competent human beings who were at least as intelligent and devout as we are today. I assume that they were quite capable of accurately interpreting their own experience and of objectively presenting what they heard and experienced in the language of their historical community, which we today can understand with due diligence. On the divine side, I assume that God has been willing and competent to arrange for the Bible, including its record of Jesus, to emerge and be preserved in ways that will secure His purposes for it among human beings worldwide. Those who actually believe in God will be untroubled by this. I assume that He did not and would not leave His message to humankind in a form that can only be understood by a handful of late-twentieth-century professional scholars, who cannot even agree among themselves on the theories that they assume to determine what the message is.[5]

Fitting the Pieces Together

The first qualification for judging any piece of
workmanship from a corkscrew to a cathedral
is to know what it is—what it was intended
to do and how it was meant to be used.

C.S. LEWIS

I want to make two major points in this book: First, that the Bible presents a unified story, the individual pieces of which are best understood in light of the whole; and second, that the story itself is quite subversive and allows for no equivocation in our response. We either submit ourselves to it or submit it to ourselves. There is absolutely no middle ground.

But this leaves several questions unanswered, and we want to wrestle with one in this chapter: How are we to fit the pieces of the Bible together in a way that makes sense? Anyone who has started to read the Bible knows that some parts are hard to understand, seemingly absurd, or offensive to modern ears. Even in New Testament times, the apostle Peter warned that some of the teachings in Paul's inspired writings "contain some things that are hard to understand, which ignorant and unstable people distort, as they do the other Scriptures, to their own destruction" (2 Peter 3:16).

With so many seemingly contradictory interpretations, with so many different groups who claim to have the only correct understanding of the Bible, do you and I have any hope of coming to a sane understanding of what it says? I will offer some practical suggestions for fitting the pieces of the Bible together along the narrative arc we have explored.

On Its Own Terms

The most important place to begin when approaching the Bible is to read it on its own terms. This means several things. First, reading the scriptures should be an exercise in our submission to God. We don't read simply for information but also for formation. We read so the scriptures will shape us to be more and more like Christ. We sit under the authority of the Bible when we read it and allow it to define us and our lives in this world. Our goal isn't to master the scriptures, but to be mastered by them. Spiritual formation is not measured by how much we know about the Bible or how often we read the Bible, but by the way we follow Jesus. This is the bottom line. We can be familiar with much of the Bible and still not love or follow Jesus. The scriptures are to set the agenda for us, not vice versa.

This means the Bible has authority over us. It is the most trustworthy gauge of what is real and true and good and beautiful. In submitting to it, we place ourselves under God's good government. The Bible is not only a trustworthy account of and testimony to His redemptive work in the world but also a part of that redemptive work.

This also means we must distinguish between exegesis (discovering the meaning of a text) and eisegesis (reading a meaning into the text). The Bible's meaning is determined by what the authors intended to convey to their original audiences. Our job is to discover that meaning, not to create it. We don't read meaning into the text on the basis of our own opinions or ideas. Rather, we let it speak for itself. We work at hearing it through the ears, hearts, and minds of those who first heard it.

Some people object that we cannot find objective meanings in Bible texts. They insist we are blinded by our own subjective constructions:

our cultural conditioning, our background presuppositions, our fallibility as human beings, and so on. I certainly agree we are incapable of perfectly objective transpersonal knowledge, but I take very seriously God's intent to communicate and reveal Himself to us in ways that get through to us despite our constructions. I am convinced God has ensured that we can obtain reliable and useful knowledge about who He is and how He works.

Most of all, the Bible is a book we are to *live* in our real lives, real relationships, real jobs, real annoyances, and real pleasures. As Jesus said, "If you hold to my teaching, you are really my disciples. Then you will know the truth, and the truth will set you free" (John 8:31-32). Unless we step into the truth it proclaims and the world it unveils, we miss its message entirely. For the last few decades the unwritten assumption in our churches has been that knowing more will equate with growing more to be like Jesus. Certainly that is partially true; true and accurate knowledge about God is the foundation of our lives. But growth in Christ requires more than correct information. We must step into the information we have in order to have what the Bible calls faith.

It Is for Them Before It Is for Us

This is our starting point if we are to understand the scriptures. I can't stress enough the importance of this truth for twenty-first-century Christians. Before we play the "what does this verse mean to me" game, we need to discover what it would have meant in its original context.

Christians commonly assume that anyone should be able to pick up a Bible and understand it without much background knowledge. This is true, to a point. The Bible is utterly and absolutely clear on the big picture—creation, fall, redemption, and restoration—even if readers don't know all the particulars. Anyone can read it and benefit in that regard. But our modern world and its cultural assumptions are vastly different from the ancient world and its cultural assumptions. So a fundamental tenet in putting the story together is to understand that it was for them before it was for us. Here is what this means.

In many important ways, the Bible is *personal*. A personal God (He gives us His name) presents Himself to persons and enters into covenant relationships with them. Accordingly, all scripture is personal in the sense that it is revelatory and not only informational. We read the scriptures differently than we read an owner's manual, list of instructions, or a textbook—even a theology textbook. The Bible focuses on God's pursuing and redeeming work among us.

Because of this, God has spoken to us in ways we can understand. He has condescended to us because we cannot grasp His greatness with our own unaided effort or understanding. He has revealed Himself in human language and categories that were common at the time. The New Testament, for instance, was written in the common, street-level, ordinary Greek of the day and not in the more polished classical Greek that scholars and poets used. Idioms, symbols, figures of speech, systems of measurement, and references to nature that were common to ancient Near Eastern folks appear in the Bible. This is the human element in scripture. It was written in particular language in a particular cultural setting, reflecting particular cultural customs and conventions and ways of thinking in order to be a word on target for the original intended audiences. This is a necessary consequence of God incarnating Himself. The human dimension of scripture is essential for it to be scripture.

This is precisely where we must do our homework. Our modern literary and cultural assumptions are often completely different from ancient ones. We expect precision in timing, dating, and quotes. Ancients had far less exacting standards. We think (without thinking) the text should conform to modern conceptions of what is appropriate, real, or literally true.

Ancient authors felt no hesitation in arranging their material in ways that best suited their purposes. Some biblical genealogies, for example, omit names and generations to achieve multiples of seven.

Matthew lists 14 generations (7 x 2) from David to the exile, and Luke records 21 (7 x 3). Both genealogies are true according to the conventions of their time.

The gospel writers arranged their material in unique ways. Mark arranged his material mostly chronologically. Matthew follows Mark's chronology but arranges the material around five major discourses by Jesus. Luke groups material together thematically, and John ordered his gospel theologically around seven signs that Jesus is the Messiah. To impose modern requirements of exact chronology on these ancient authors leads to all sorts of distortion. Their main goal was to reveal the character of the people they wrote about, so they included things that served that end—even things of little historical consequence. The apostle John admits as much at the end of his gospel:

> This is the disciple who testifies to these things and who wrote them down. We know that his testimony is true. Jesus did many other things as well. If every one of them were written down, I suppose that even the whole world would not have room for the books that would be written (John 21:24-25).

Under the guidance of the Holy Spirit, John selected from many stories about Jesus and topics in His teaching. Each gospel writer had to pick and choose in this way. This doesn't mean that the gospels aren't true; it simply means that each author arranged and presented his material in a way that helped him make his point.

In some cases, the writers needed to change some words in order to communicate one meaning to many different people. Thus Luke has "Glory in the highest" where Matthew and Mark have "Hosanna in the highest." *Glory* made better sense to Luke's Gentile (non-Jewish) audience than *hosanna.*

Sometimes authors paraphrase or rearrange words. Mark and Luke quote Jesus talking about the kingdom of *God,* but Matthew quotes Jesus talking about the kingdom of *heaven.* Matthew, a Jew writing to

Jews, used the substitute for *God* because Jews usually avoided using God's name for fear of taking it in vain. (Many still do.)

These examples can be multiplied. Here's the point: The main reason we misunderstand the Bible is that we read it with our modern expectations and presuppositions, trying to understand a first-century text in a twenty-first-century way. We are not in the position of the ancient Israelites or early Christians. These texts were clear to the people who wrote them and (mostly) clear to the readers as well. But for them to be clear for us, we must enter into their worlds, their forms of writing and speaking, their ways of conveying important truths. It is not enough to roughly translate their words into English and then just assume we should be able to understand what they say and mean. We must seek to understand the Bible on its own terms and its own turf, from inside its world and not from our own.

The book of Revelation was written to encourage and strengthen seven flesh-and-blood first-century churches when the emperor Domitian was persecuting Christians. The book was *for them,* and John even says so: "Blessed is the one who reads the words of this prophecy, and blessed are those who hear it and take to heart what is written in it, because the time is near" (Revelation 1:3). This assumes it would have been understood by those who originally received it.

So when Revelation describes an evil empire, a ruler named 666, or a beast from the sea, it is not talking about Saddam Hussein, Iraq, or the European Union. The earliest Christians recognized that John used imagery and symbols that hinted at the Roman Empire and the emperor.

Pay Attention to Genre

One of the keys to reading and making sense of the Bible's story is to understand that it uses different kinds of literature, and each kind has different rules that govern its use. The word *genre* refers to literary categories, such as narrative history, law, instruction, and poetry. The text could also be a letter, a sermon, a prophecy, a prayer... Each type of literature sends its own signals as to how to understand it, and each requires a different approach. If we don't ask ourselves questions about the genre of a passage—what kind of literature it is and what kind of information it contains—we are bound to misunderstand and misuse that part of the Bible. We must interpret different kinds of literature in different ways. To understanding the big story of the Bible, we must pay attention to clues about the genre of each part.

But if we are to pay attention to different genres, are we not to read the entire Bible literally? Generally speaking, yes we should. Even though the Bible contains a variety of literary genres and many figures of speech, the biblical authors most often used literal statements to convey their ideas. But perhaps the word *literal* is no longer helpful in discussions about the Bible. Rather, we should read the Bible *literarily*, according the type of literature it is. If an ancient account of history says that Jesus went to a particular place and did a particular thing, I read it as history. But when I read about the good Samaritan, I don't wonder about his name because I'm reading a parable. I recognize that Jesus is telling a story to illustrate a moral point and that stories like this rarely claim to correspond to actual events.

The Story Unfolds Progressively

Another key to putting the pieces of the Bible together is to understand that it is one gradually unfolding story and that Christ is the thread that ties the whole thing together. We cannot begin to understand the individual pieces of the story apart from the whole. The purity laws of Leviticus make no sense apart from God's purposes in creation and redemption. The confident and seemingly "too good to be true" proverbs promising success and wealth to the obedient are balanced by the epic narrative of Job, which seems to delight in dismantling such formulas about God and man, obedience and sin, blessing and suffering. Every part of the Bible has a purpose (even the genealogies), but we are most likely to discover that purpose by considering how each part fits in the overall story. When we dissect the scriptures into bite-sized snippets, we are on the way to making them say something they were never intended to say.

We must also remember that the story unfolds progressively.

> In the past God spoke to our forefathers through the prophets at many times and in various ways, but in these last days he has spoken to us by his Son, whom he appointed heir of all things, and through whom he made the universe (Hebrews 1:1-2).

The idea of progressive revelation has profound implications. For one thing, it reminds us to consider the earlier parts of the story in the light of what comes after. Each part of the story was way ahead of the culture it was written in. Even many of the puzzling passages of the Old Testament that seem outdated or offensive to us were redemptive and progressive compared to the law and practice of other nations. But still, God didn't drop the whole thing down from heaven all at once. Each piece of the Bible invites us to take another step toward God's original and unchanging intent for us: flourishing human lives participating in the good reign and rule of our Creator. We see this when comparing the Old Testament with the Sermon on the Mount (Matthew 5–7). The Old Testament law limiting vengeance—"Eye for eye, and tooth for tooth" (Exodus 21:24; Leviticus 24:20; Deuteronomy 19:21)—was revolutionary for its day, as was Jesus' interpretation of it:

> You have heard that it was said, "Eye for eye, and tooth for tooth." But I tell you, Do not resist an evil person. If someone strikes you on the right cheek, turn to him the other also. And if someone wants to sue you and take your tunic, let him have your cloak as well. If someone forces you to go one mile, go with him two miles. Give to the one who asks you, and do not turn away from the one who wants to borrow from you (Matthew 5:38-42).

The same is true with the law about murder and Jesus' application to anger, the law about adultery and Jesus application about lust, and the law about vows and Jesus' instruction to avoid making them in the first place. The commands have a redemptive trajectory that we must keep in mind. Often this trajectory includes *recapitulation* (the word means "to do over again"). Many events in scripture foreshadow things to come. For instance, the sacrificial system, the priesthood, and the temple all prefigured the person and work of Jesus (Hebrews 5; 8–10). Paul refers to Jesus as the second Adam, which is a way of saying Jesus is reversing Adam's sin and its effects. Jesus recapitulates the Exodus narrative by leading a new Israel on a new exodus.[1] Israel's vocation (Exodus 19:5-6) is now given to the church (1 Peter 2:5,9). We could cite many more examples of this.[2] Here's the point: A careful reading of the big story reveals that we need all the parts if we are to make the fullest sense of the whole.

The Center of the Story

We have seen that the author of Hebrews alludes to the fact that God has spoken in many ways to His people—through visions, dreams, commands, law, prophets, and more—but now speaks definitively through the revelation of His Son. God revealed Himself partially or piecemeal in the past, but fully and finally now in the Son. The incarnate Word is God's most crucial revelation of Himself, and all the earlier revelations prepare for it and foreshadow and anticipate it. Jesus Himself becomes the centerpiece of the story; all the parts revolve around Him, as Luke and John both make clear:

> Now that same day two of them were going to a village called Emmaus, about seven miles from Jerusalem. They were talking with each other about everything that had happened. As they talked and discussed these things with each other, Jesus himself came up and walked along with them; but they were kept from recognizing him.

He asked them, "What are you discussing together as you walk along?"

They stood still, their faces downcast. One of them, named Cleopas, asked him, "Are you only a visitor to Jerusalem and do not know the things that have happened there in these days?"

"What things?" he asked.

"About Jesus of Nazareth," they replied. "He was a prophet, powerful in word and deed before God and all the people. The chief priests and our rulers handed him over to be sentenced to death, and they crucified him; but we had hoped that he was the one who was going to redeem Israel. And what is more, it is the third day since all this took place. In addition, some of our women amazed us. They went to the tomb early this morning but didn't find his body. They came and told us that they had seen a vision of angels, who said he was alive. Then some of our companions went to the tomb and found it just as the women had said, but him they did not see."

He said to them, "How foolish you are, and how slow of heart to believe all that the prophets have spoken! Did not the Christ have to suffer these things and then enter his glory?" And beginning with Moses and all the Prophets, he explained to them what was said in all the Scriptures concerning himself (Luke 24:13-27).

He said to them, "This is what I told you while I was still with you: Everything must be fulfilled that is written about me in the Law of Moses, the Prophets and the Psalms."

Then he opened their minds so they could understand the Scriptures. He told them, "This is what is written: The Christ will suffer and rise from the dead on the third day, and repentance and forgiveness of sins will be preached in his name to all nations, beginning at Jerusalem. You are

> witnesses of these things. I am going to send you what my
> Father has promised; but stay in the city until you have been
> clothed with power from on high" (Luke 24:44-48).

> You diligently study the Scriptures because you think that
> by them you possess eternal life. These are the Scriptures
> that testify about me, yet you refuse to come to me to have
> life (John 5:39-40).

"The Law of Moses, the Prophets, and the Psalms" is a Jewish
synonym for the entire Old Testament. Jesus came as the pinnacle,
fulfillment, and climax of the story that began with the God's call
to Abraham. Matthew begins his gospel by fixing Jesus at the center
of Israel's story: "A record of the genealogy of Jesus Christ the son of
David, the son of Abraham."

From before creation to the end of the world, Jesus' presence is
center stage.

> In the beginning was the Word, and the Word was with
> God, and the Word was God. He was with God in the
> beginning (John 1:1).

> Behold, I am coming soon! My reward is with me, and
> I will give to everyone according to what he has done. I
> am the Alpha and the Omega, the First and the Last, the
> Beginning and the End (Revelation 22:12-13).

Note that in Luke 24, quoted above, Jesus tells the disciples that
the scriptures are inspired because they speak of Him. Jesus is not a
character in the Bible. He is not a couple of chapters in the book. He is
the story. He is the fullest and clearest revelation of God. He is the central
character of the drama and the one who reverses the entire human
situation. The authors of the Bible reach for language big enough to
describe the exalted Christ:

- "The Son is the radiance of God's glory and the exact

representation of his being, sustaining all things by his powerful word" (Hebrews 1:3).

- "He is the image of the invisible God, the firstborn over all creation. For by him all things were created: things in heaven and on earth, visible and invisible, whether thrones or powers or rulers or authorities; all things were created by him and for him. He is before all things, and in him all things hold together. And he is the head of the body, the church; he is the beginning and the firstborn from among the dead, so that in everything he might have the supremacy. For God was pleased to have all his fullness dwell in him, and through him to reconcile to himself all things, whether things on earth or things in heaven, by making peace through his blood, shed on the cross" (Colossians 1:15-20).

- "For in Christ all the fullness of the Deity lives in bodily form" (Colossians 2:9).

Jesus Himself said, "Anyone who has seen me has seen the Father" (John 14:9-10). God is most decisively revealed in Jesus Christ. He cannot be other than He is in Jesus. Nothing is more central to the New Testament's view of Jesus than this.

Many parts of the Bible are puzzling or seem offensive to modern ears. In those instances, we look for the big story, the redemptive arc, the biblical thread of redemption and restoration. But we also fix our eyes on Jesus, the author and perfecter of our faith. He is the point. When I am unsure about God's actions or commands, I am willing to suspend my judgment because of who Jesus is. When I struggle to understand a difficult piece of theology, I am willing to humble myself and trust Jesus like a child because of how amazing He is. My faith isn't in the Bible; my faith is in *Him*. And because my faith is primarily in Him, my faith is also in the Bible. John Stott makes this point well:

Christians are not, or ought not to be, what we are sometimes accused of being, namely, "bibliolaters," worshippers of the Bible. We do not worship the Bible; we worship the Christ of the Bible...

A young man who is in love [has] a girlfriend who has captured his heart. As a result he carries a picture of his beloved in his wallet because it reminds him of her when she is far away. Sometimes, when nobody is looking, he might even take the photograph out and give it a surreptitious kiss. But kissing the photograph is a poor substitute for the real thing. And so it is with the Bible. We love it only because we love him of whom it speaks.[3]

Other Lights to Navigate By

We have many other tools that can help us put together the story of the Bible. The Bible is remarkably clear and unified, especially considering that it's a collection of 66 books that dozens of authors and editors wrote and compiled across a span of a thousand years. But making sense of some of the individual parts (using the top of the puzzle box to help us arrange the pieces, to refer back to our metaphor) takes a bit of work. Whole books address each of these points, but these highlights will point us in the right direction:

- If we take the scriptures seriously, we will submit to them as the highest authority over our lives and our believing communities. If God was somehow involved in their composition and compilation, the Bible can hold no lower position. This means, at the very least, that when the Bible addresses something clearly (leaving minimal room for interpretation), we will prioritize what the scriptures say about that issue or topic above our own personal preferences or subjective experiences and above contemporary popular assumptions and opinions. To take the Bible seriously in this way is to take God's authority over us seriously also.

- Clear parts of the Bible help us understand unclear parts of the Bible. We should look at the whole story before rendering judgment on individual parts. This, of course, assumes a single unifying mind behind the whole thing. Also, we need to keep this principle in tension with the idea of progressive revelation we discussed earlier. The story unfolds over the course of time, so older parts may be renewed, fulfilled, or supplanted by newer parts, and we must determine which of the older parts are to be carried forward as we find our place in the story today.

- From Ben Witherington: "Reason, tradition [how the Bible has been interpreted throughout the ages by God's people], and experience can all be seen as windows into the Scripture or avenues out of the Scripture by which we may express the truth of Scripture, but in no case and on no occasion should reason, tradition, or experience be seen as a higher authority than Scripture by which Scripture could be trumped *on some issue that Scripture clearly addresses* and about which it makes claims on God's people."[4]

- Just in case I haven't said it enough already: The best way to understand the individual parts of the Bible is to engage the entire story. For example, we cannot rightly understand the New Testament apart from the Old Testament and vice versa.

- We must ask at least five questions of any passage of the Bible:

1. What was the author's intent, and who is his audience? As we have said, the Bible has dual authorship. It is both human and divine. So we must ask what God and the human authors—Moses, Ezekiel, Paul, Matthew, or others— intended when they wrote or edited their texts and gave them to Israel or the early church. We need to understand the meaning of the words the author uses and the way he

employs them in the text. We need to try to reconstruct the culture and readership he addresses. This is a difficult task, for it requires a healthy respect for the distance (culturally, socially, linguistically) between the text and us. We must be careful to travel back in time, so to speak, to grasp, the best we can, some idea of how the original audience might have heard this. Some resources to help are listed at the end of this book.

2. What is the genre of the passage in question? What kind of literature and literary forms within it are we studying? Is this poetry or prose? History or law? Story or parable? Psalm or proverb? Apologetics or liturgy? Prophecy or apocalyptic? Different types of literature require different kinds of reading. The best introduction to the issues of genre is *How to Read the Bible for All Its Worth* (third edition) by Gordon D. Fee and Douglas Stuart (Grand Rapids, MI: Zondervan, 2003).

3. Where does this passage (and its context) fit in the overall story of the Bible? This is critical and will help avoid many misunderstandings.

4. What prior assumptions, values, and worldview commitments do we bring to the study of this text? If we assume we are objective, free from biases or prejudices, we are fooling ourselves. We all come to the text with frameworks for understanding that are largely unconscious, at least until they are exposed. The only way to deal with this carefully is to admit it and then try to uncover the worldview that is presupposed and articulated in the text we are studying.

I have found that reading or studying the Bible with someone from a third-world country is a great way to expose the Western perspective I bring to the Bible. Reading commentaries written by Africans, South Koreans, or messianic Jews (and others) helps too. Moreover, as N.T. Wright has said, studying the Bible requires a "hermeneutic of love." God speaks to His faithful as they are humble before Him. Prayer, worship, and Bible study, even critical study, must go together. The same Spirit who revealed the text works in us to illumine our minds, lead our hearts to worship, and empower our wills to obey.

5. Once we have determined the meaning of a text, what implications open up? For example, when Paul says, "Do not get drunk on wine," the meaning is clear. But the implications include, "Don't get drunk with whiskey, don't get drunk with gin, don't get high on drugs." Did Paul know that when he wrote? No. What Paul knew was that wine intoxicates us; we are not to be under its influence (out of control), but under the influence of the Spirit (responsibly in control). These other intoxicants can be implied because they are consistent with Paul's intent.

The study of scripture requires much from us, and perhaps that is why so many of us settle for the one-minute Bible or the "what does this verse mean to me" approach to it. God can and does speak to anyone with a humble heart—even using these methods, but a much richer reward awaits those willing to put in the effort.

The Story of Israel

*When the past is lost, as it now is in our Western
world, there is nothing left to focus on except the self.*

ROBERT E. WEBBER

M any of us struggle to make sense of the Old Testament. The
obscure laws, the repetitious geneologies, the half-crazed visions
of the prophets, and the seemingly endless stories about Israel's rebellion, judgment, and rescue all contribute to our tenuous relationship
with (or avoidance of) the first parts of the Bible story.

The Story Line of the Old Testament, Part I

The Pentateuch (the first five books of the Bible) gives us the foundation for the biblical worldview. Without it we can lapse into false
understandings. For instance, a second-century group (the Gnostics)
tried to sever the Old Testament from the New Testament and edited
the New Testament accordingly. Here's the result: Creation is evil, to be
redeemed is to free one's soul from the prison of the body, Jesus is not
God incarnate, and seekers can find God through a secret wisdom. The
church rejected this as false teaching. They realized that the Hebrew
scriptures were so central to Christian faith, all future attempts to
eliminate the Old Testament constituted an attack on that faith.

I want to use the first five books of the Old Testament (particularly Genesis) to illustrate what we miss by not working to explore, understand, and interpret the Hebrew Bible (what the Jews—and those sensitive to them—call the Old Testament).[1]

Genesis means "origin," from the Greek translation of the opening of Genesis 1:1—"In the beginning." This is the book of origins: the origin of the universe, its order and complexity, the solar system, the atmosphere, life, humanity, marriage, evil, language, government, culture, nations, revealed faith, the chosen people… Everything starts here. In order to understand the end, we must understand the beginning.

In Genesis we learn that the sovereign God, in His freedom, created the heavens and the earth—space, time, nature, history, human beings. All are created by Him and for Him. We also learn of the original goodness of creation, which is now marred by the fall. Genesis hints that a heavenly revolt stained earth when our first parents were seduced into rebellion against God. Scripture opens with a cosmic, wide-angle view: All things were created by God and are now fallen. The panorama shrinks to a pinpoint focus as God begins His rescue plan by calling one man, Abraham. The vista will gradually grow as God blesses first Abraham, then his descendents, then the nation they grow into, and then the nations of the world. Eventually the entire creation will be restored, and God will be all in all.

Genesis shows us that nature, history, and the entire Bible are eschatological (that is, they are concerned with "last things"). The days of creation climax in the seventh day—the Sabbath, the day of rest. As biblical revelation unfolds, this becomes a sign and a metaphor for the day of salvation. Adam and Eve, though judged by the fall, receive the promise of ultimate victory over their enemy (Genesis 3:15). In the fullness of biblical revelation, Adam points beyond himself to the second Adam (Jesus), through whom God begins a whole new race of the redeemed.

The biblical story operates in a twofold way. First, it tells us the truth about God and nature, history and humanity, sin and redemption.

Second, and at the same time, it stands against and subverts all other stories. The Genesis account of creation breaks down the ancient alternatives, which hold that history is cyclical and determined by cosmic myths, that the earth is the battleground of the gods and is subject to the rise and fall of the Nile or the cycles of nature. Biblical revelation formed the Western worldview (providing the impetus for science, medicine, and the arts) for roughly 1500 years.

Genesis gives us the background and presuppositions for the Exodus from Egypt, which N.T. Wright calls "the controlling narrative" of the Bible. As the great book of redemption, Genesis tells us who Yahweh is: He is the one true God, the Creator of all things, who remembers His covenant with Abraham and delivers His nation from Pharaoh so they can receive their inheritance and be a people after His heart for the sake of the nations. In other words, redemption is a step in God's rescue plan to restore the cosmos to His creative purpose. He also shows Himself true to His promise to bless the nations through Abraham.

Genesis shows us that God is the Creator and that His creation is good. It is the arena for His glory (see Psalms 8; 19). Creation is worth redeeming. There is no dualism between matter and spirit here. That is, we cannot say that physical things are bad and spiritual things are good. As in the ancient world, so today, Genesis challenges alternative worldviews. Genesis subverts the naturalism of Darwin, which claims that nature moves according to the laws of natural selection, producing the survival of the fittest. (Social Darwinism applies this to business, politics, and other areas of human relationships.) Through mutation, nature evolves from the simple to the complex. The process of evolution is mindless, not governed by God or any other outside power.

Genesis also challenges the monism of Hinduism. God is the Creator, and creation is not an illusion. It is temporal, but it is real. The goal of salvation is not to escape nature and history but to participate in its renewal and restoration in the new heaven and new earth.

The Story Line of the Old Testament, Part 2

By Jesus' day, the Old Testament was divided into three sections—the Law, the Prophets, and the Writings.[2] The Law is the first five books of the Old Testament (also called the Law of Moses, the book of Moses, or the Pentateuch). The Prophets are divided into two categories: major (longer) and minor (shorter). And finally, the writings include the Psalms and the wisdom literature (Proverbs, Job, Song of Songs, Ecclesiastes). Today, we organize the Old Testament into three units: historical books (the first 17 books, from Genesis to Esther), wisdom and poetry (the middle 5 books, from Job through Song of Songs), and prophetic books (the last 17 books, Isaiah to Malachi). This arrangement is easy to understand, but it jumbles up the material a bit so that the historical continuity of the story is harder to discern.

The key for our purposes (and this changed the way I read and understood the Old Testament) is that almost all of the story line of the Old Testament narrative is found in 11 books. Reading these books in succession helps us understand the historical flow of the story of Israel and the way the other Old Testament books fit in. Here are the 11 books: Genesis, Exodus, Numbers, Joshua, Judges, 1 and 2 Samuel, 1 and 2 Kings, Ezra, and Nehemiah. And here's a very short historical summary of each:

- Genesis moves from creation to the death of Joseph in Egypt.
- Exodus begins with the birth of Moses and ends with the construction of the tabernacle at Mt. Sinai.
- Numbers covers the wilderness journey from Mt. Sinai to the very edge of the Promised Land.
- Joshua presents Israel's conquest of the promised land and ends with the death of Joshua.
- Judges covers the 400-year period of Israel's life in Canaan and the continued cycle of rebellion, judgment, rescue that ensues.

- First Samuel introduces Israel's transition from a tribal federation to a monarchy under Saul.

- Second Samuel narrates King David's reign.

- First Kings moves from Solomon's reign to the division of the kingdom.

- Second Kings follows the divided kingdoms until their exile.

- Ezra tells the story of some of the Jews' return from Babylon to the promised land and the rebuilding of the temple.

- Nehemiah covers the Jews' life back in the Promised Land, including the rebuilding of the walls of Jerusalem.

The rest of the books of the Old Testament fit into this historical story line. They do not advance the plot but rather fill it out.

- Leviticus (situated during the time of the book of Exodus) provides details about the covenant and how Israel was to live it out in God's presence.

- Deuteronomy (situated during the time covered in Numbers) is Moses' last sermon to the Israelites before they entered the Promised Land. (It summarizes Exodus and Numbers.)

- First and 2 Chronicles summarizes much of 1 and 2 Samuel and 1 and 2 Kings. It is written to Israel after the exile (so it is situated during the time of Ezra and Nehemiah).

- Ruth (situated during the period of Judges) and Esther (situated during exile in Babylon) remind God's people of His faithfulness to them in the darkest days of their history.

- The books of wisdom and poetry (Job through Song of Songs) fit generally within the period narrated by 1 and 2 Kings and reflect the experience of God's people as they live in covenant relationship with Him.

- The prophetic books were written before, during, and after

the exile and remind Israel of its covenant obligations to
God and His corresponding blessings and judgments.

What About All Those Weird Commandments?

In the book of Leviticus, God gives Israel some commands that
are downright odd to modern readers. Understanding the purpose
behind some of them will allow us to see how even the most esoteric
parts of the Old Testament story fit into the overall structure we have
been examining: creation, fall, redemption, restoration. To understand
some of the obscure commandments in Leviticus, we must do a little
background first.

God's unconditional and perpetual covenant with Abraham is at
the forefront as Israel suffers in bondage in Egypt.

> The Israelites groaned in their slavery and cried out, and
> their cry for help because of their slavery went up to God.
> God heard their groaning and he remembered his cove-
> nant with Abraham, with Isaac and with Jacob. So God
> looked on the Israelites and was concerned about them
> (Exodus 2:23-25).

God calls Moses, against his objections, to return to Egypt and
lead the people out so they might worship Him. God promises to be
with Moses and to perform signs and wonders to validate him and
to deliver Israel. Sprung from Egypt and carrying the spoils of battle,
Israel is delivered through the Red Sea and brought to Sinai. Yahweh,
the triumphant King, now comes down on the smoking mountain to
visit His people and establish a new covenant with them. It is modeled
on the Hittite vassal treaty and differs from the royal-grant covenant
to Abraham in two respects. First, it is conditional and temporal. If
the Israelites obey, they will be blessed. If they disobey, they will be
cursed. Second, Yahweh is free to revoke the covenant at any time.
He is the great King, and Israel is His vassal state.

God establishes two central institutions at Sinai: the Torah and the tabernacle (which later becomes the basis for the temple). The Israelites are to live in obedience to God and worship Him appropriately. The Torah (the teaching of the books of Moses) orders the Israelites' life and prepares them to live in the Promised Land. It contains both personal and social legislation, the moral and ritual law. The central summary is found in the Ten Commandments in Exodus 20. God's overwhelming concern in this legislation is that Israel would have no other gods before Him. Idolatry was the great threat to Israel's life. God called the nation to be a holy people, to worship and serve only Yahweh as a witness to nations filled with superstition and darkness.

Through the Old Testament, we learn that Yahweh is sovereign over all of Israel's life. In every aspect, the people are to live in obedience to Him. The ritual law (covered in both Exodus and Leviticus) not only regulates access to Yahweh through the priesthood and sacrifice but also orders the calendar year around three great feasts that celebrate the fruitfulness of the land and the exodus events. When the tabernacle is completed according to God's specifications, His glory comes and fills it. "Then the cloud covered the Tent of Meeting, and the glory of the LORD filled the tabernacle. Moses could not enter the Tent of Meeting because the cloud had settled upon it, and the glory of the LORD filled the tabernacle" (Exodus 40:34-35). This is Israel's uniqueness: Yahweh is present with His people. Moses tells the Lord...

> If your Presence does not go with us, do not send us up from here. How will anyone know that you are pleased with me and with your people unless you go with us? What else will distinguish me and your people from all the other people on the face of the earth? (Exodus 33:15-16).

God's people are to live in His presence, in the memory of their redemption from Egypt, and in the hope of God's covenant promise to Abraham for the sake of the nations to bless the whole earth.

The Pentateuch is clear about our continuing sin and need of grace.

The other nations around Israel are stuck in persistent superstition and idolatry. As the story unfolds, Israel is hardly any better. God's people are in regular rebellion. Moses goes up the mountain, and the people below make a golden calf. Hardship comes, and they want to go back to Egypt. They refuse the short route into the Promised Land and spend 40 years in the wilderness until that generation has died off. Even Moses fails to enter the land he sees. As we have said above, the whole of biblical history is eschatological. The institutions of the tabernacle, the sacrifice, the priesthood and festivals, the legislation demanding faithfulness and obedience, the promise of a prophet like Moses who will come (Deuteronomy 18:15)—all of these point to the future. The Pentateuch, like the rest of the Old Testament, is a story in search of an ending—the kingdom of God fully realized and restored in a new world.

With this backdrop in mind, we can now consider some of the reasons why (we think) God commanded the things He did. For instance, the laws regarding clean and unclean animals could have simply helped keep the community healthy. The majority of animals that were prohibited from Israel's consumption were more likely to carry disease, they were harder to raise in the desert and the Promised Land, and they were used by the surrounding nations for religious sacrifices.

One purpose of the purity system was to maintain Israel's distinctiveness (Leviticus 11:44-45). Many of the commands kept Israel distinguishable from the surrounding nations so the people could fulfill their identity as the ones God chose to display to the world what He is like. Two of the most obscure and difficult-to-understand commandments fall into this category: "Do not cook a young goat in its mother's milk" (Deuteronomy 14:21) and "Do not mate different kinds of animals... Do not wear clothing woven of two kinds of material" (Leviticus 19:19). The Israelites were not to behave like other people in ways that were religiously or morally reprehensible. Not mixing cotton and wool reminded Israel not to mix their religious life with the other nations' idolatrous and despicable worship practices. The instructions themselves emphasize the importance of making distinctions, of keeping things separate.

Why should this matter? Leviticus 20:24-26 provides the answer. Clean animals were to be distinct from unclean animals, just as Israel was to be distinct from other peoples. God evidently intended these practices to express Israel's calling to be separate from other peoples. Israel was to be distinct from other peoples even in ways that did not matter religiously or morally, because they could fulfill God's purpose for them (to foreshadow and lead up to the Messiah) only if they were a separate people. This is why the system was abolished in the New Testament (Acts 10).

These and other prohibitions were designed to forbid the Israelites to engage in the fertility cult practices of the Canaanites. These pagan tribes thought that boiling a goat kid in its mother's milk would magically ensure the continuing fertility of the flock. Mixing animal breeds, seeds, or materials supposedly married and magically produced offspring, or agricultural abundance. God refused to sanction such idolatry and superstition. The Israelites' faithfulness to their covenant responsibilities and God's corresponding blessing of them were the keys to Israel's safety and provision.

We could look at many more examples, but knowing the general intention that applied to many of the laws helps us see them as central to Israel's life as God's chosen people and to their vocation as a light to the nations. God is not arbitrary, but gracious and beneficial.

Where To Next?

*If the knowledge we acquire through our reading
and study of this text that involves us in following
Jesus, diverts us from the very Jesus we started out
following, we would have been better off never
to have opened the book in the first place.*

EUGENE PETERSON

I hope you are seeing that you can view the Bible in many ways but that they are not all equal. There are some ways, some fostered by the church, that contribute to its seeming irrelevance to modern life. But there are other ways to read it—often articulated by poets, artists, storytellers, and hands-on theologians and pastors and mystics—that cause it to come alive to us again. I have tried to paint a picture of the subversive nature of the Bible, of its way of telling an alternative story about what is real and true, so that we may once again see the scriptures as something to be immersed into, a story to be lived, a breathtaking vista that opens up whole worlds of possibility. Many questions remain unanswered, so I have listed other resources at the end of this chapter. But I want to end by simply exploring the practical implications of approaching the Bible in this way. Robert Webber gets us started:

- God's *narrative* is the one true story of the world.

- The church's *mission* is to be a witness to God's narrative of the world (*missio Dei*).

- *Theology* is the church's corporate reflection on God's narrative.

- *Worship* sings, proclaims, and enacts God's narrative to the glory of God.

- Individual *spirituality* is the personal embodiment of God's narrative in all of life.

- Collective *spirituality* is the church's embodied life in the world.[1]

As we saw in chapter 15, the assumptions, agendas, and expectations we bring to the Bible are often the greatest hindrances we must overcome to understanding it more fully. Using the Bible (to win an argument, for example) is utterly different from submitting to it. We must read to be formed by the scriptures, convinced that the Bible tells the truest story of the world, that it reveals reality to us. We must come with ears to hear, to use Jesus' metaphor. Our hearts must be open, receptive, and seeking what God has in store. We approach the scriptures humbly, knowing that knowledge puffs up and that love for God and neighbor counts most of all. We must read to put ourselves under Jesus' authority and not to fulfill our own purposes and agendas. Eugene Petersen puts it well:

> Every expectation that we bring to this book is inadequate or mistaken. This is a text that reveals the sovereign God in being and action. It does not flatter us, it does not seek to please us. We enter this text to meet God as he reveals himself, not to look for truth or history, or morals that we can use for ourselves. What he has insisted upon was that we do not read the Bible in order to find out how to get God into our lives, get him to participate in our lives. That is getting it backward.[2]

As we participate in this strange new world of virgin births and parted seas and resurrections from the dead, we not only have to be willing to accept the strangeness of this world—that it doesn't fit our preconceptions and tastes—but also the staggering largeness of it. We must avoid forcing scripture to fit our experience. Our experience is too small; it is like trying to force the ocean into a thimble.

The Bible occasionally pictures its characters eating a book or scroll (Jeremiah 15:16; Ezekiel 2:8–3:3; Revelation 10:9-10). This formative reading is not merely objective rational analysis, which often allows our heads to be divorced from our lives. No, each of us should "consume" the text, allowing it to work its way inside us—way down into our guts—so that every area of life is affected. We need more than information—facts about God and ourselves. We need formation—deep change that shapes us into a certain kind of being. In the Bible, God reveals Himself and His ways to us, not so much telling us something, but *showing* Himself. This is not the impersonal reading of a phone book or encyclopedia; this is more like a widow reading old love letters from her husband.

We must read the Bible in the way it comes to us, not in the way we come to it. Our purposes in reading must give way to the Author's purposes in writing. We open our hearts to a new world and step into it right in the middle of our world's competing stories. This is a struggle; we have a hard time bowing down to any higher authority, whether human or divine. That is why our relationship to the Bible must be part of our relationship with God. One of the ways God Himself exercises authority is through His written words to us.

Suggestions for Reading

- Read s-l-o-w-l-y.
- Read large chunks of the Bible at a time. If you devote a week to reading through all four gospels, you'll notice things you never saw before. Read Exodus or Acts in one sitting.

- Listen to it on CD or MP3. The Bible was meant to be heard before it was meant to be read.

- Read it out loud.

- Take a short section (like Philippians) and read it every day for a month.

- Learn to pray as you read.

- Have a notebook handy as you read and write down anything you have questions about. Then meet with somebody and talk about it. Wrestle with it. Chew on it. Puzzle over it. Let mystery, paradox, and tension take you to Jesus.

Of course, there are many more ways to read, study, consume, and sit under the scriptures. Ultimately, what you find there usually corresponds to what you bring with you.

Creative Subversion

Nowhere does the Bible say that it alone is where God speaks. In fact, the scriptures mention many of the ways God speaks to His people. He speaks through creation (Psalm 24:1; Romans 1:18-20), visions (Ezekiel 37; Acts 9:10; 10:10-11), and dreams (Genesis 41; Daniel 2). At times He commanded His prophets to act out visual parables in order to warn Israel (Isaiah walked around naked, and Ezekiel lay on his side for 430 days, cooked food over human excrement, and shaved off his beard and hair [Isaiah 20:2-4; Ezekiel 4:4-8; 5:1-4]). God speaks through conscience (Romans 2:14-15), gospel preaching (Romans 10:14-17), and directly by the Spirit's words of knowledge, prophecy, and tongues interpreted (Acts 2:4-8; 1 Corinthians 12:8-10).

So the Bible gives us great permission to listen for God's voice both within the Bible and without. God may use anything to speak to us, so we must pay careful attention throughout our everyday lives. The biblical authors themselves borrowed from much non-Jewish and non-Christian culture as they presented the true story of God to the world.

As the biblical authors testified about Israel's God and His Messiah, Jesus, they often co-opted ancient literary conventions, art forms, or even poetry. The books of Jonah and Job share much in common with ancient epics. Some scholars suggest the book of Mark bears a striking resemblance to an Aristotelian Greek tragedy.[3] The covenants of Exodus and Deuteronomy reflect the structure and conventions of ancient Near Eastern suzerain treaties between kings and their subjects.[4]

This should not be a problem for us. Using pagan literary or art forms in no way implies that the Bible is unhistorical. It simply adapts cultural ways of communicating in order to convey religious truth. This is the art of *subversion*—the retelling of one mythology in terms of another.[5] To take the categories, thought or literary forms, or the art and poetry of one culture and use it to tell the Christian story— that is what we mean by subversion. This happens throughout the scriptures. John's use of *logos* (a Greek term referring to the rational underlying or ordering principle of the cosmos) to describe Jesus in John 1:14 is an example. The creation account of Genesis 1 contains the same motifs of separation, naming, and function that pervade Egyptian and Mesopotamian creation stories.[6] The Book of Hebrews subversively interacts with the Hellenism of the first century.[7] Even New Testament words like *gospel, Savior, Lord, peace,* and *church* are taken from Roman propaganda about the emperor and empire. Jesus Himself told stories that were subversive of Jewish teaching and expectation of that day (Matthew 21:31-44; 22:1-14; 24:45-51; 25:1-13). Paul quotes from noncanonical Jewish mythology (2 Timothy 3:8) and from pagan poets.

Jude quotes from two Jewish books, The Assumption of Moses and 1 Enoch, that were not officially sanctioned as part of the Jewish Bible. Paul quotes the Greek dramatist Menander (who was known for his raunchy productions) in 1 Corinthians 15:33 and uses imagery from the athletic contests of his day (Philippians 3:13-14) as well as the victory processions of Roman emperors (2 Corinthians 2:14-16;

Colossians 2:15). In Acts 17 Paul retells the pagan story of the world (currently popular at the time) within a Christian framework.[8] In so doing he systematically refutes the major points of Stoic beliefs. He does not quote a single Old Testament text to these philosophers, but he regularly quoted scripture when preaching to the Jews (Acts 26:22-23; 28:23-28). Instead, he quotes Epimenides and Aratus, Greek poets who wrote praising Zeus. Paul subverts their concept of God by giving common terms new definitions to undermine their entire narrative. When a biblical author quotes an outside source, it does not mean that the author agrees with everything that source said or wrote. It does mean that some statements of truth are made outside the scriptures by those who may not even know God.

Part of our duty as we improvise the fifth and final (and unfinished) act in the drama of the Bible (in Wright's framework) is to immerse ourselves in the one true story as well as the other stories of our culture. Paul obviously exposed himself to the pagan art and culture of his day. He seems to have studied them—to be able to quote them and take advantage of their narrative. He redemptively interacted with those categories and belief systems. Paul quoted a poem about Zeus to make the case for Jesus. He told an *alternative story.* He used his hearers' thought forms, images, and poetry, and he showed how they pointed to the ultimate story of Jesus' coming into the world. We must watch out for accommodation in doing this, of course (compromising the true story so it doesn't subvert other stories). It is a very real danger. When we creatively subvert something, we take its stories, images, and symbols and redefine them in ways that point to Jesus. And this, I want to suggest, is what is called for also today. Richard John Neuhaus summed all this up nicely when he wrote, "The church and its gospel throw into question the agenda of the world—all the agendas of the world—and open the world to possibilities of which it has never dared to dream. When the church dares to be different, it models for the world what God calls the world to become."[9]

Afterword

Let the word of Christ dwell in you richly.

Colossians 3:16

My hope and prayer is that you might be inspired toward the scriptures and read them for yourself. It does take work to dig around inside of them, making sense of ancient codes and laws, wisdom and poetry, prophesy and song. But the work is well worth it, and every single bit of it is there for a reason. Through His written word, God invites us to see the world as He would have us see it, to renew our minds and break out of the shapes and patterns of this world that mold us.

I encourage you to read the Bible again with fresh eyes and an open and humble heart. Much current, popular Bible teaching must be filtered and tested by the real thing. I love the way Paul puts it (when speaking of prophecy): "Test everything. Hold on to the good" (1 Thessalonians 5:21). This is good advice today. We must start asking, if we were on a desert island, and all we had was the Bible, what would we believe about…

the church

the Holy Spirit

the gifts of the Holy Spirit

sexuality

humanity

God

salvation[1]

I am convinced that many of us would change our thinking about these things if all we had were the scriptures. We must constantly be wary of what Robert Webber calls *theological legalism*—protecting the faith by adding to it. It often goes beyond biblical faith and practice and requires adherence to systems of belief and behavior that go beyond the scriptures and the freedom that Jesus has given us to live a new life in Him. Webber gives some examples:

> All evangelicals agree that the Bible is the final authority in matters of faith and practice; legalism adds that biblical authority can be expressed only with full, plenary, verbal inspiration of the Bible.
>
> All evangelicals agree that God is the Creator; legalists add a literal interpretation to Genesis 1 and insist that Scripture teaches that God created the world in seven days.
>
> All evangelicals believe in the church; legalists insist that their church or fellowship is the pure church and all others are apostate.
>
> All evangelicals believe in the second coming of Christ; legalists insist that their particular view of the end time (i.e., pretribulation rapture and pre-millenialism) is the one true understanding of Scripture.[2]

You may or may not agree with Webber's examples, but the point remains that like the Pharisees, we can move beyond what the scriptures clearly teach. I think many today are told what "the Bible says" without checking it out for themselves. This should change, I think. If we didn't have church history, seminaries, Bible teachers—and we had only the Bible itself—what would we come to think, believe, and live? I want to be clear: church history, seminaries, and Bible teachers can be (and often are) helpful and (sometimes) even necessary. But far too many of us just settle for listening to various authorities and never dive in ourselves. If we take the Bible seriously, we must constantly seek to let it define us, not the other way around.

Dorothy Sayers makes this point beautifully. A scientist once asked her to write a letter to his scientific organization, explaining her reasons for believing in the Christian faith. The letter was not at all what the scientist had expected:

> Why do you want a letter from me? Why don't you take the trouble to find out for yourselves what Christianity is? You take time to learn technical terms about electricity. Why don't you do as much for theology? Why do you never read the great writings on the subject, but take your information from the secular "experts" who have picked it up as accurately as you? Why don't you learn the facts in this field as honestly as in your own field? Why do you accept mildewed old heresies as the language of the church, when any handbook of church history will tell you where these came from? Why do you balk at the doctrine of the Trinity—God the Three in One—yet meekly acquiesce when Einstein tells you $E = MC^2$? What makes you suppose that the expression "God ordains" is narrow and bigoted, while your own expression "Science demands" is taken as an objective statement of fact? You would be ashamed to know as little about internal combustion as you know about Christian beliefs.
>
> I admit you can practice Christianity without knowing much theology, just as you can drive a car without knowing much about internal combustion. But when something breaks down in the car, you go humbly to the man who understands the works; whereas, if something goes wrong with religion, you merely throw the works away and tell the

theologian he is a liar. Why do you want a letter from me telling you about God? You will never bother to check on it or find out whether I'm giving you personal opinions or Christian doctrines. Don't bother with me. Go away and do some work and let me get on with mine.[3]

Resources

Do you need a general and basic introduction to understanding the Bible? Here are some to choose from.

Fee, Gordon D., and Douglas Stuart. *How to Read the Bible for All Its Worth,* third ed. Grand Rapids: Zondervan, 2003.

————. *How to Read the Bible Book by Book.* Grand Rapids: Zondervan, 2002.

Fee, Gordon D., and Mark L. Strauss. *How to Choose a Translation for All Its Worth.* Grand Rapids: Zondervan, 2007.

Do you have questions about how the Bible came together? Here are two basic ones:

Arnold, Clinton E. *How We Got the Bible: A Visual Journey.* Grand Rapids: Zondervan, 2008.

Geisler, Norman L., and William E. Nix. *From God to Us: How We Got Our Bible.* Chicago: Moody Press, 1974.

These two are for intermediate readers:

McDonald, Lee Martin. *The Biblical Canon: Its Origin, Transmission, and Authority.* Peabody: Hendrickson, 2007.

Wegner, Paul D. *The Journey from Texts to Translations: The Origin and Development of the Bible.* Grand Rapids: BridgePoint Books, 1999.

These three are more advanced:

Bruce, F.F. *The Canon of Scripture.* Downers Grove: InterVarsity Press, 1988.

Evans, Craig A., and Emanuel Tov, eds. *Exploring the Origins of the Bible:*

Canon Formation in Historical, Literary, and Theological Perspective. Grand Rapids: Baker Academic, 2008.

Metzger, Bruce M. *The Canon of the New Testament: Its Origin, Development and Significance.* Oxford: Clarendon Press, 1987.

Do you wonder whether the gospels record what actually happened? Here are three good basic books:

Habermas, Gary R. *The Historical Jesus: Ancient Evidence for the Life of Christ.* Joplin: College Press, 1996.

Komoszewski, J. Ed, M. James Sawyer, and Daniel B. Wallace. *Reinventing Jesus: How Contemporary Skeptics Miss the Real Jesus and Mislead Popular Culture.* Grand Rapids: Kregel, 2006.

Strobel, Lee. *The Case for Christ: A Journalist's Personal Investigation of the Evidence for Jesus.* Grand Rapids: Zondervan, 1998.

Here are three good intermediate options:

Bock, Darrell L., and Daniel B. Wallace. *Dethroning Jesus: Exposing Popular Culture's Quest to Unseat the Biblical Christ.* Nashville: Thomas Nelson, 2007.

Perrin, Nicholas. *Lost in Transmission? What We Can Know About the Words of Jesus.* Nashville: Thomas Nelson, 2007.

Wilkins, Michael J., and J.P. Moreland, eds. *Jesus Under Fire: Modern Scholarship Reinvents the Historical Jesus.* Grand Rapids: Zondervan, 1995.

And here are three advanced approaches:

Blomberg, Craig L. *The Historical Reliability of John's Gospel: Issues and Commentary.* Downers Grove: InterVarsity Press, 2001.

_____. *The Historical Reliability of the Gospels.* Downers Grove: InterVarsity Press, 1987.

Witherington III, Ben. *What Have They Done with Jesus?: Beyond Strange Theories and Bad History—Why We Can Trust the Bible.* New York: HarperSanFrancisco, 2006.

Do you have questions about difficult passages in the Bible? Check out this book:

Kaiser Jr., Walter C., Peter H. Davids, F.F. Bruce, and Manfred T. Brauch. *Hard Sayings of the Bible.* Downers Grove: InterVarsity, 1996.

Do you have questions about books that were not included in the Bible?

Bock, Darrell L. *The Missing Gospels: Unearthing the Truth Behind Alternative Christianities*. Nashville: Thomas Nelson, 2006.

Evans, Craig A. *Fabricating Jesus: How Modern Scholars Distort the Gospels*. Downers Grove: InterVarsity, 2006.

Strobel, Lee. *The Case for the Real Jesus: A Journalist Investigates Current Attacks on the Identity of Christ*. Grand Rapids: Zondervan, 2007.

Could you use some guidance on how to read the Bible?

Foster, Richard J. *Life with God: Reading the Bible for Spiritual Transformation*. New York: HarperOne, 2008.

Longman III, Tremper. *Reading the Bible with Heart and Mind*. Colorado Springs: NavPress, 1997.

Peterson, Eugene H. *Eat This Book: A Conversation in the Art of Spiritual Reading*. Grand Rapids: Eerdmans, 2006.

Stott, John. *The Contemporary Christian: Applying God's Word to Today's World*. Downers Grove: InterVarsity, 1992.

Do you need some help understanding the Old Testament?

Dillard, Raymond B., and Tremper Longman III. *An Introduction to the Old Testament*. Grand Rapids: Zondervan, 1994.

Hill, Andrew E., and John H. Walton. *A Survey of the Old Testament,* second ed. Grand Rapids: Zondervan, 2000.

Kaiser Jr., Walter C. *The Old Testament Documents: Are They Reliable and Relevant?* Downers Grove: InterVarsity, 2001.

Longman III, Tremper. *Making Sense of the Old Testament: Three Crucial Questions*. Grand Rapids: Baker Academic, 1998.

Motyer, Alec. *The Story of the Old Testament,* Grand Rapids: Baker Books, 2001.

Wright, Christopher J.H. *The Mission of God: Unlocking the Bible's Grand Narrative*. Downers Grove: IVP Academic, 2006.

Yancey, Philip. *The Bible Jesus Read*. Grand Rapids: Zondervan, 1999.

Do you have questions about how to interpret the Bible? Here are two basic resources:

Russell, Walt. *Playing with Fire: How the Bible Ignites Change in Your Soul*. Colorado Springs: NavPress, 2000.

Sproul, R.C. *Knowing Scripture,* rev. ed. Downers Grove: InterVarsity, 2009.

Here are four intermediate options:

Carson, D.A. *Exegetical Fallacies,* second ed. Grand Rapids: Baker Academic, 1996.

Duvall, J. Scott, and J. Daniel Hays. *Grasping God's Word: A Hands-On Approach to Reading, Interpreting, and Applying the Bible,* second ed. Grand Rapids: Zondervan, 2005.

Fee, Gordon D. *New Testament Exegesis: A Handbook for Students and Pastors,* third ed. Louisville: Westminster John Knox Press, 2002.

Stuart, Douglas. *Old Testament Exegesis: A Handbook for Students and Pastors,* third ed. Louisville: Westminster John Knox Press, 2001.

These three books are more advanced:

Bock, Darrell L., and Buist M. Fanning, eds. *Interpreting the New Testament Text: Introduction to the Art and Science of Exegesis.* Wheaton: Crossway Books, 2006.

McKnight, Scot, ed. *Introducing New Testament Interpretation.* Grand Rapids: Baker Books, 1989.

Osborne, Grant R. *The Hermeneutical Spiral: A Comprehensive Introduction to Biblical Interpretation,* second ed. Downers Grove: InterVarsity, 2006.

Do you want to understand more about the Bible as a story and why that matters?

Bartholomew, Craig G., and Michael W. Goheen. *The Drama of Scripture: Finding Our Place in the Biblical Story.* Grand Rapids: Baker Academic, 2004.

_____. *Living at the Crossroads: An Introduction to Christian Worldview.* Grand Rapids: Baker Academic, 2008.

Vanhoozer, Kevin J. *The Drama of Doctrine: A Canonical Linguistic Approach to Christian Theology.* Louisville: Westminster John Knox Press, 2005.

Are you interested in some of the historical background of the Old and New Testaments?

Burge, Gary M., Lynn H. Cohick, and Gene L. Green. *The New Testament in Antiquity: A Survey of the New Testament Within Its Cultural Contexts.* Grand Rapids: Zondervan, 2009.

Gundry, Robert H. *A Survey of the New Testament,* fourth ed. Grand Rapids: Zondervan, 2003.

Jeffers, James S. *The Greco-Roman World of the New Testament Era: Exploring the Background of Early Christianity.* Downers Grove: InterVarsity, 1999.

Keener, Craig S. *The IVP Bible Background Commentary: New Testament.* Downers Grove: InterVarsity Press, 1993.

Scott Jr., J. Julius. *Jewish Backgrounds of the New Testament.* Grand Rapids: Baker Academic, 1995.

Walton, John M., Victor H. Matthews, and Mark W. Chavalas. *The IVP Bible Background Commentary: Old Testament.* Downers Grove: InterVarsity, 2000.

Bibliography

Bartholomew, Craig G., and Michael W. Goheen, *The Drama of Scripture: Finding Our Place in the Biblical Story.* Grand Rapids: Baker Academic, 2004.

Bertrand, J. Mark. *(Re)Thinking Worldview: Learning to Think, Live, and Speak in This World.* Wheaton: Crossway Books, 2007.

Donner, Theo. "Some Thoughts on the History of the New Testament Canon," Themelios 7.3, April 1982: 23-27.

Erickson, Millard J. *Christian Theology,* second ed. Grand Rapids: Baker, 1998.

Hirsch, Alan, and Michael Frost. *The Shaping of Things to Come: Innovation and Mission for the 21ˢᵗ-Century Church.* Peabody: Hendrickson, 2003.

Godawa, Brian. *Word Pictures: Knowing God Through Story and Imagination.* Downers Grove: InterVarsity Press, 2008.

Grudem, Wayne. *Systematic Theology: An Introduction to Biblical Doctrine.* Grand Rapids: Zondervan, 1994.

Hegeman, David Bruce. *Plowing in Hope: Toward a Biblical Theology of Culture.* Moscow, ID: Canon Press, 1999.

Longman III, Tremper. *Reading the Bible with Heart and Mind.* Colorado Springs: NavPress, 1997.

Lucas, James R. *Knowing the Unknowable God: How Faith Thrives on Divine Mystery.* Colorado Springs: WaterBrook Press, 2003.

McKnight, Scot. *The Blue Parakeet: Rethinking How You Read the Bible.* Grand Rapids: Zondervan, 2008.

Peacock, Charlie. *New Way to Be Human: A Provocative Look at What It Means to Follow Jesus.* Colorado Springs: Shaw Books, 2004.

Petersen, Eugene H., *Eat This Book: A Conversation in the Art of Spiritual Reading.* Grand Rapids: Eerdmans, 2006.

Plantinga Jr., Cornelius. *Engaging God's World: A Christian Vision of Faith, Learning, and Living.* Grand Rapids: Eerdmans, 2002.

_____. *Not the Way It's Supposed to Be: A Breviary of Sin.* Grand Rapids: Eerdmans, 1995.

Ryken, Leland, James C. Wilhoit, and Tremper Longman III, eds. *Dictionary of Biblical Imagery.* Downers Grove: InterVarsity Press, 1998.

Tchividjian, Tullian. *Unfashionable: Making a Difference in the World by Being Different.* Colorado Springs: Multnomah Books, 2009.

Vanhoozer, Kevin J., Charles A. Anderson, and Michael J. Sleasman, eds. *Everyday Theology: How to Read Cultural Texts and Interpret Trends.* Grand Rapids: Baker Academic, 2007.

Webber, Robert E. *The Divine Embrace: Rediscovering the Passionate Spiritual Life.* Grand Rapids: Baker Books, 2006.

_____. *Who Gets to Narrate the World? Contending for the Christian Story in An Age of Rivals.* Downers Grove: InterVarsity Press, 2008.

Witherington III, Ben. *The Living Word of God: Rethinking the Theology of the Bible.* Waco: Baylor University Press, 2007.

Wittmerchael, E. *Heaven Is a Place on Earth: Why Everything You Do Matters to God.* Grand Rapids: Zondervan, 2004.

Wright, John W. *Telling God's Story: Narrative Preaching for Christian Formation.* Downers Grove: InterVarsity Press, 2007.

Wright, N.T. *The New Testament and the People of God.* Minneapolis: Fortress Press, 1992.

_____. *The Last Word: Beyond the Bible Wars to a New Understanding of the Authority of Scripture.* New York: HarperSanFrancisco, 2005.

_____. *Simply Christian: Why Christianity Makes Sense.* New York: HarperSanFrancisco, 2006.

Notes

Chapter 1: The True Story of the World

1. Leland Ryken, James C. Wilhoit, and Tremper Longman III, eds., *Dictionary of Biblical Imagery* (Downers Grove: InterVarsity Press, 1998), 91-92.

2. N.T. Wright, *The New Testament and the People of God* (Minneapolis: Fortress Press), 40, 78. On the question of whether or not Paul utilizes narrative in his letters, see pages 77-80.

3. Kenneth E. Bailey, *Jacob and the Prodigal: How Jesus Retold Israel's Story* (Downers Grove: InterVarsity Press, 2003), 51; quoted in Brian Godawa, *Word Pictures: Knowing God Through Story and Imagination* (Downers Grove: InterVarsity Press, 2008), 69.

4. Wright, *The New Testament and the People of God,* 38-40.

5. John W. Wright, *Telling God's Story: Narrative Preaching for Christian Formation* (Downers Grove: InterVarsity Press, 2007), 82.

6. See Mike Erre, *Death by Church* (Eugene: Harvest House, 2009); see also Craig G. Bartholomew and Michael W. Goheen, *The Drama of Scripture: Finding Our Place in the Biblical Story* (Grand Rapids: Baker Academic, 2004), 24-25.

7. N.T. Wright, "How Can the Bible Be Authoritative?" *Vox Evangelica,* no. 21, 1991, 7-32; see also Wright, *The New Testament and the People of God,* 139-43.

8. Bartholomew and Goheen, *The Drama of Scripture,* 25-26.

9. Ibid., 26.

10. Ibid.

Chapter 2: The Beginning and the Time Before That

1. Bartholomew and Goheen, *The Drama of Scripture,* 37.

2. "In Genesis 4 we read about Cain and the city called Enoch, Jabal (the ancestor of those who live in tents and keep livestock), Jubal (the ancestor of those who play the lyre and pipe), Tubal-Cain (who made all kinds of bronze and iron tools), and Lamech (who wrote poetry). Not all of this cultural activity was sinful—it was part of the cultural mandate given to our first parents. These cultural achievements are what God had in

mind for us all along—God made the world with the human potential for imaginative, artistic activity. Cultural activity is a fundamental way in which we serve and glorify God" (Bartholomew and Goheen, *The Drama of Scripture*, 48-49).

3. The Hebrew word translated *helper* has no trace of inferiority or subordination. The word is actually used of God in several places in the Old Testament. A parallel translation based on these incidents could be *rescuer*. The last part of verse 18 reads literally, "I will make for him a helper as in front of him (or according to what is in front of him)." This last phrase, "as in front of him (or according to what is in front of him)" occurs only here and in verse 20. It suggests that what God creates for Adam will correspond to him. The woman will be neither superior nor inferior, but equal. The Hebrew word for *helper* is masculine, though here it describes the woman. This word cannot denote an associate or subordinate status because it usually describes Yahweh's relationship to Israel. He is Israel's help(er) because He is the stronger one. See, for example, Exodus 18:4; Deuteronomy 33:7,26,29; Psalms 33:20; 115:9-11; 124:8; 146:5.

4. Cornelius Plantinga Jr., *Not the Way It's Supposed to Be: A Breviary of Sin* (Grand Rapids: Eerdmans, 1995), 10.

Chapter 3: The God-Absented World

1. Bartholomew and Goheen, *The Drama of Scripture*, 31.

2. Ibid.

3. Bertrand Russell, "A Free Man's Worship," in *Why I Am Not a Christian*, ed. by Paul Edwards (New York: Simon & Schuster, 1957), 107. Quoted in J.P. Moreland, *The God Question* (Eugene: Harvest House, 2009), 40.

4. Craig M. Gay, *The Way of the (Modern) World* (Grand Rapids: Eerdmans, 1998), 19. Quoted in Moreland, *The God Question*, 156.

5. Moreland, *The God Question*, 29.

6. Philip Cushman, "Why the Self Is Empty," *American Psychologist* 45, May 1990, 600. Quoted in Moreland, *The God Question*, 32-33.

7. Peter Singer, *Practical Ethics* (New York: Cambridge University Press, 1979), 122-23.

Chapter 4: The Twisting of Everything Good

1. Bartholomew and Goheen, *The Drama of Scripture*, 42.

2. He makes sure Noah and his family are rescued—along with animals, showing that God is concerned with all of creation. Salvation doesn't stop with humankind; it embraces the whole of creation (Romans 8:21; Jonah 4:11).

3. Plantinga, *Not the Way It's Supposed to Be*, 5.

4. In Genesis 3:20, God provides for Adam and Eve's shame, clothing them with the skins of animals. In the Old Testament, to remove someone's clothes could signify their disinheritance; God's provision of clothes for Adam and Eve is a sign to them that He has not given up on His purpose for them. They are still to bear His image in the world and steward the earth. See Bartholomew and Goheen, *The Drama of Scripture*, 44.

Chapter 5: Echoes and Ashes: The Vandalism of *Shalom*

1. Malcolm Muggeridge, "Jesus: The Man Who Lives," in *Seeing Through the Eye: Malcolm Muggeridge on Faith*, ed. Cecil Kuhne (San Francisco: Ignatius Press, 2005), 16.

2. Cornelius Plantinga Jr., *Engaging God's World: A Christian Vision of Faith, Learning, and Living* (Grand Rapids: Eerdmans), 64.

3. Robert E. Webber, *Who Gets to Narrate the World? Contending for the Christian Story in an Age of Rivals* (Downers Grove: InterVarsity Press, 2008), 29.

4. Plantinga, *Engaging God's World,* 79.

5. Michael W. Goheen and Craig G. Bartholomew, *Living at the Crossroads: An Introduction to Christian Worldview* (Grand Rapids: Baker Academic), 2008, 47.

6. J. Mark Bertrand, *(Re)Thinking Worldview: Learning to Think, Live, and Speak in This World* (Wheaton: Crossway Books, 2007), 87.

Chapter 6: The Cosmic Rescue Operation

1. Bartholomew and Goheen, *Living at the Crossroads,* 51.

2. God confronts Pharaoh, who defies Him (Exodus 5:2). The plagues clearly show who has supreme power, because each confronts an Egyptian deity, as God explicitly declares (Exodus 12:12). The plagues show that what the Egyptians think to be true of their gods is actually true of the Lord God of heaven and earth. Pharaoh himself was regarded as divine—the son of the sun god, Re. As a god, Pharaoh was responsible for maintaining what the Egyptians called *ma'at,* or order in the creation. When the cosmic order goes wrong, the plagues show Pharaoh's inability to maintain *ma'at.* Instead, Yahweh and His agents (Moses and Aaron) overcome in the cosmic struggle, demonstrating who really controls for forces of nature so that God's name might be proclaimed in all the earth (Exodus 9:16). See Bartholomew and Goheen, *The Drama of Scripture,* 63.

3. Terence E. Fretheim, "Exodus," in *Interpretation: A Bible Commentary for Preaching and Teaching* (Louisville: John Knox, 1991), 263. Quoted in Bartholomew and Goheen, *The Drama of Scripture,* 72.

4. The rise and fall of the kingship is told in three Old Testament two-part books (1 and 2 Samuel, 1 and 2 Kings, and 1 and 2 Chronicles).

5. At the end of the Old Testament, the Israelites' future remains uncertain. They are back in the land with the rebuilt temple, but neither the nation nor the temple are what they were (Haggai 2:3). Most of the prophets focused on Israel's situation at the time they were writing, but before, during, and after the exile, they also spoke of what was to come. They pictured Israel's future in terms of its past, using terms like *son of David* and *Mount Zion* and focusing on the temple and on Israel as God's servant. Their messages often emphasized that God would judge Israel. His glory and renown among the nations was at stake in Israel's life, so He could not tolerate their rebellion forever. See Bartholomew and Goheen, *The Drama of Scripture,* 111.

6. Bartholomew and Goheen, *The Drama of Scripture,* 137-38:

   > When Jesus heals the blind (Lk. 18:35-43), the lame (Mk. 2:1-12), the mute and deaf (7:31-36), and the leper (Luke 17:11-19), people see God's healing and renewing power flowing into human history to end the reign

of sickness and pain. When Jesus calms the sea (Mk. 4:35-41), feeds the hungry (8:1-10), and prepares an extraordinary catch of fish of weary fishermen (Luke 5:1-11), he demonstrates the power of God to renew and restore a cursed creation. When he raises Lazarus (John 11), the widow's son (Lk. 7:11-17), and Jarius's daughter (Mk. 5:21-43), the people see the power of god conquering even death. Not only does Jesus display God's power to liberate humanity from the ravages of death, evil and suffering; he also shows God at work to heal the entire creation. These miracles are like windows through which we catch glimpses of a renewed cosmos, from which Satan and his demons have been cast out.

Chapter 7: The Offense of the Cross

1. Peter Kreeft, *Making Sense out of Suffering* (Ann Arbor: Servant Books, 1986), 132.

Chapter 8: The Beginning of the End and the End of the Beginning

1. The Greek word that designates the newness of the new cosmos is not *neos,* but *kainos*. *Neos* means new in time or origin, whereas *kainos* means new in nature or quality. *New* here means renewed rather than brand new. See Bartholomew and Goheen, *The Drama of Scripture,* 231, note 2, and Michael E. Wittmer, *Heaven Is a Place on Earth: Why Everything You Do Matters to God* (Grand Rapids: Zondervan, 2004), 205.

2. Wittmer, *Heaven Is a Place on Earth,* 188.

3. N.T. Wright, *Paul for Everyone: 1 Corinthians* (Louisville: Westminster John Knox Press, 2004).

Chapter 9: Life After Life After Death

1. Kevin J. Vanhoozer, Charles A. Anderson, and Michael J. Sleasman, eds., *Everyday Theology: How to Read Cultural Texts and Interpret Trends* (Grand Rapids: Baker Academic, 2007), 219.

2. N.T. Wright, *Surprised by Hope: Rethinking Heaven, the Resurrection, and the Mission of the Church* (New York: HarperOne, 2008), 219.

3. Wittmer, *Heaven Is a Place on Earth,* 17.

4. Tullian Tchividjian, *Unfashionable: Making a Difference in the World by Being Different* (Colorado Springs: Multnomah Books, 2009), 50.

5. Wittmer, *Heaven Is a Place on Earth,* 74.

Chapter 10: A New Way of Seeing the World

1. Dallas Willard, unpublished talk.

2. For more on this see Dallas Willard, *Knowing Christ Today* (New York: HarperOne, 2009).

3. Dallas Willard, *The Divine Conspiracy* (New York: HarperSanFrancisco, 1998), 320. See also Dallas Willard, *Hearing God* (Downers Grove: InterVarsity Press, 1999), 156-57.

4. I am indebted to J.P. Moreland for these three points.

5. Willard, *Hearing God,* 154.

6. Eugene H. Peterson, *Eat This Book: A Conversation in the Art of Spiritual Reading* (Grand Rapids: Eerdmans, 2006), 4.

Chapter 11: Stepping into God's Story

1. Bartholomew and Goheen, *The Drama of Scripture,*13.

2. Wright, "How Can the Bible Be Authoritative?" Wright sees the story in five acts: creation, fall, Israel, Jesus, and church. I have suggested a different framework: creation, fall, redemption, and restoration. Wright's structure has the advantage of more clearly drawing out our place in the story.

3. Ibid.

4. For more on what a disciple is and does, see Willard, *The Divine Conspiracy.*

Chapter 12: Our Place in the Story

1. Alan Jones, *Soul Making* (New York: Harper & Row), 166. Quoted in Tremper Longman III, *Reading the Bible with Heart and Mind* (Colorado Springs: NavPress, 1997), 30.

2. John Frame, *The Doctrine of the Christian Life* (Phillipsburg: P &R, 2008), 861-62.

3. Wittmer, *Heaven Is a Place on Earth,* 121.

Chapter 13: The Kind of Story It Is

1. James R. Lucas, *Knowing the Unknowable God: How Faith Thrives on Divine Mystery* (Colorado Springs: WaterBrook Press, 2003), 20.

2. Of course, this doesn't prove that the Bible is inspired. It only shows that the authors claimed that it was.

3. Gordon D. Fee, *Gospel and Spirit: Issues in New Testament Hermeneutics* (Peabody: Hendrickson, 1991), 30-34.

4. Frederick Buechner, *Wishful Thinking* (San Fransico: HarperCollins, 1993), 9. Quoted in Longman, *Reading the Bible with Heart and Mind,* 93.

5. Willard, *The Divine Conspiracy,* xvii.

Chapter 14: Fitting the Pieces Together

1. See Erre, *Death by Church.*

2. For more examples, see Robert E. Webber, *The Divine Embrace: Rediscovering the Passionate Spiritual Life* (Grand Rapids: Baker Books, 2006), 127-40.

3. John R. W. Stott, in James Hewett, *Illustrations Unlimited* (Wheaton: Tyndale House), 1988, 44. Quoted in Longman III, *Reading the Bible With Heart and Mind,* 45.

4. Ben Witherington III, *The Living Word of God: Rethinking the Theology of the Bible* (Waco: Baylor University Press, 2007), 160-61.

Chapter 15: The Story of Israel

1. The material of this section relies heavily on unpublished work by Don Williams.

2. The material that follows comes from a class I had in seminary: Genesis to Malachi: A Survey of Old Testament History and Literature, class notes, Dr. David Talley, Biola University, Talbot School of Theology.

Chapter 16: Where To Next?

1. Webber, *Who Gets to Narrate The World?* 124.

2. Peterson, *Eat This Book,* 67.

3. Godawa, *Word Pictures,* 64.

4. Erre, *Death by Church,* 500.

5. Godawa, *Word Pictures,* 109. *Mythology* simply refers to the body of stories associated with a culture or institution.

6. Godawa, *Word Pictures,* 116.

7. Godawa, *Word Pictures,* 141 and following.

8. Godawa, *Word Pictures,* 121, 133.

9. Quoted in Tchividjian, *Unfashionable,* 80.

Afterword

1. I am indebted to Francis Chan for this point.

2. Webber, *The Divine Embrace,* 82.

3. Dorothy Sayers, "*Christianity Today,* vol. 25, no. 21, December 11, 1981).

It's a Harsh,
Crazy,
Beautiful,
Messed Up,
Breathtaking
World...

And People Are Talking About It...